1997

to Margaret
with Love
Edgar Brooks

BACK TO
BUCK LAKE

BACK TO BUCK LAKE

For the sake of the
outdoor sportsmen,
world-renowned taxidermists,
Edgar and Allie Brooks
have now told their story

S. Lowell Roberts

Eastern Itascan Company
Nashwauk, Minnesota

Book Design by Joyce Peraaho

*Photographs from the Brooks' scrapbook reproduced by
Tribune Graphic Arts, Hibbing, Minnesota*

COPYRIGHT © 1993 by Edgar J. Brooks and Allie Brooks

First Edition

Published by arrangement with
Edgar J. Brooks and Allie Brooks

Library of Congress Catalog Card No. 93-071649

ISBN: 0-9636894-0-1

Published in the United States of America by
Eastern Itascan Company
310 Central Avenue
Nashwauk, Minnesota 55769

Distributed by
Edgar J. and Allie Brooks
3911 Fourth Avenue East
Hibbing, Minnesota 55746
(218) 262-2575

PRINTED IN THE UNITED STATES OF AMERICA

To Marjorie

I expect to pass through this life but once;
Therefore, any good that I can do,
Any kindness that I can show,
Let me do it now;
For I shall not pass this way again.
                                    —ANONYMOUS

Contents

Prologue ix

A Unique Couple
  1 First impressions 3
  2 Buck Lake hospitality........... 17
  3 Bright idea 29

Edgar's Story
  4 Where there's trouble 43
  5 Coming to Buck Lake 63

Allie's Story
  6 Take care of yourself 81
  7 For better, for worse 93

A Consuming Habit
  8 First homestead 103
  9 Last resort 125
  10 Hunter's paradise............... 145

The American Dream
  11 Lives in transition 161
  12 A business is born 173
  13 Satisfaction guaranteed....... 193
  14 People business.................. 207
  15 Escaping the drudgery 221

The Golden Years
  16 Return to Buck Lake........... 245
  17 Elixir of life 255
  18 Caring touch 271

Scrapbook 281

Prologue

Basically, *Back To Buck Lake* is a biography of two people. It is predicated upon, not only what they have done, but what they are currently doing to make the world a better place for their having lived in it.

My wife and I first met the Brooks family back in July of 1940, at which time they resided on a small farm located in the rural bush country only a few miles from their retirement home on Buck Lake.

We renewed our acquaintanceship with them during a brief stop-over at their place of business in Minneapolis in 1962. Then once again, after the passage of 29 years, we had occasion to pay them a third visit in August of 1991.

It was during the later occasion of visitation that my attention was drawn to a hard-cover ring binder scrapbook lying at random on the large oak table in their dining room.

Perusing its contents, out of curiosity, I soon found myself swept up in an aura of intrigue with the voluminous collection of pictures, newspaper clippings and personal letters, depicting their 30 years in the taxidermy business in Minneapolis—an epic, in its own right, that comprises more than half of the scrapbook.

I was enthralled to an even greater extent at the incredible volume of memorabilia having to do with Edgar and Allie's involvement, after their retirement from business, in providing a unique style of musical entertainment for senior citizens living in the Iron Range territory of northeastern Minnesota.

The establishment of their husband-and-wife musical combo, known throughout their entire area as "Edgar and Allie's Coo-Coo Band," has proven itself to be another exciting and meaningful chapter in the lives of this enterprising couple.

"God has blessed us richly," Edgar volunteered when I had completed my study of the scrapbook. "I sometimes have to pinch myself to determine whether all the good things that have happened to Allie and me, including the host of friends we have made from all walks of life, is for real or only a dream.

"We've sort of decided it is only fitting that we devote our Golden Years to trying to bring a little ray of sunshine and joy into the lives of folks less fortunate than us. They are in abundance all around us here in northern Minnesota, to be sure, and that's what Edgar and Allie's Coo-Coo Band is all about—to try to put back at least some of the blessings that we have received."

What follows is a humble endeavor on my part, as the author of this biography, to share with the world just how this fantastic couple has gone about doing just that.

—S. LOWELL ROBERTS

A
Unique
Couple

1

First impressions

In the strictest sense of the word, this story could well have its commencement on Edgar Brooks' birthday on January 9, 1916. However, the actual forces that culminated themselves in the eventual undertaking to write this biography of Edgar and his wife, Allie, were conceived on a Saturday night in a small town in north central Iowa on July 3, 1940.

True to the tradition of the time and area, the business district of Clarion, the county seat of Wright County, Iowa, was abuzz with a goodly representation from the surrounding farm community, as well as that of at least a small percentage of the town's citizenry. The former were in town to purchase the needed groceries and other sundry items to carry them through the upcoming week. The latter were mingling with the milling throng of people, young and old, largely out of curiosity or, in some instances, to take advantage of the opportunity to visit with friends from the rural area. Friends were almost certain to be found amongst the parade of shoppers that filled the sidewalk from curb to storefronts throughout the three-block expanse of the business district. These urban residents were here, despite the fact that it was expedient for them to walk or drive the relatively short distance from their homes to procure their needed items on any given day of the week. This luxury was not always the case with the farm folk living beyond the city limits.

Equally true to tradition, and seemingly impervious to the socializing on the part of the teeming pedestrians, was the bumper-to-bumper parade of autos of diverse vintage, occupied by young folks, male and female, traversing the entire length of the main street in both directions. The ongoing traffic cycle required U-turns at each extremity of the three-block course, only to resume the traditional pastime in the opposite direction.

The evening was wearing on, with the hands of the illuminated clock on the courthouse tower resting on 9 o'clock, when my wife and I, in the company of another young couple with whom we had been closely associated for several years, decided to duck into the New Home Cafe on Main Street for a cup of coffee and a light snack of some kind.

"What have you guys got planned for the Fourth of July?" Marion Robinson inquired when we had positioned ourselves in a convenient booth.

"Hadn't given the matter much thought," I responded. "Nothing specific, I guess."

"How would you and Jo like to drive up to northern Minnesota and spend the holiday visiting some relatives of Betty's who live way up in the boondocks near Hibbing? If we start now, we can be there by tomorrow morning."

All of us had been up since early morning, busily engaged in our respective vocations; Marion and Betty as farmers and I as a route salesman for a well-known household supply company.

The seed of Marion's impromptu suggestion found fertile soil in young adventurous minds and within a matter of minutes, the idea had taken root.

"Do you have any fishing tackle?" Marion inquired of me.

"No, but I can fix that damned quick," I responded.

Before the hour was up, the aforementioned fishing equipment had been purchased at Shupe's Hardware Store, minimal arrangements incidental to the 400-mile trip had been made, and the four of us were underway in my recently-purchased new Plymouth sedan.

For Jo and me, at least, this sort of thing represented an unanticipated adventure of challenging proportions. Out-of-state trips had been a rare occurrence for either of us.

During the itinerary between Clarion and Minneapolis, the excitement of our sudden undertaking tended to wave off any sense of drowsiness. But as the night wore on, it became a matter of necessity to keep up a steady exchange of chatter as our eyelids grew heavier with each passing mile.

By the time our entourage had crossed the

state line and entered Minnesota, Marion and Betty had filled Jo and me in on considerable background having to do with Betty's relatives, whom we were planning to visit without having granted them the common courtesy of any prior announcement that we were coming.

We learned that Fred Brooks, a brother of Betty's father, had migrated to northern Minnesota from Wright County, Iowa, during the Great Depression of the Thirties. As with many families during the prosperous Twenties, the nation-wide economic collapse, heralded by the stock market crash in 1929, had resulted in devastating reverses in Fred's financial well-being—reverses that had wiped out nearly all of his somewhat vast holdings almost overnight.

As our foursome motored northward through the dark of night, the highlights of the Brooks' move to Itasca County, in the heart of the Iron Range, were touched upon by our hosts, not only to provide a familiarity with the setting we would be encountering upon our arrival, but as a means of combating the need for sleep, now manifesting itself among all four of us.

Fred Brooks, the story continued to unfold, had traded a ballroom—one of the few assets he had managed to salvage—for a sizable parcel of unimproved land a few miles north of Nashwauk in the vicinity of Buck Lake.

Transporting their belongings by rail to Nashwauk in the dead of winter, Fred, along with his wife, Ina, and their three children, had lived in a heated tent in town until later the following spring.

It has been said that the capacity for adapting to change is the secret of survival; and during those sometimes distress-filled weeks and months of that first winter in their new surroundings, these newly-arrived pioneers from

Iowa had gallantly risen to the occasion. Needless to say, the transition from the comfortable way of life to which they had become accustomed, to that in which they had now been forced, was harsh, indeed.

As a family project, when the severest of the winter months had passed, the task of clearing off that portion of their land needed to construct a house and barn upon was commenced in earnest. Since the lumber required for the erection of these buildings was readily available from the virgin timber on their own property, the acquisition of a sawmill with which to convert these felled trees into dimension lumber was pursued and accomplished.

By the time the following winter had arrived, two things of major significance had been achieved: A comfortable home for Fred's family, set back a short distance from the highway, had been built; and a thriving sawmill business had been established, drawing its patronage from neighbors with building needs similar to his own.

The preponderance of the local residency at that time was made up of families of Finnish extraction who had migrated into the region several generations prior to the arrival of Fred Brooks and his family. One such family, the Peratalo family, lived only a few miles from the Brooks' homestead. Their children attended the same school as the Brooks children; and it was there that Edgar Brooks and Allie Peratalo—the latter became Edgar's wife—first met.

As we motored northward through the long night, Marion divulged the fact that he had spent a month or so as a guest of the Brooks family during the prior winter. Along with Edgar and several of Allie's family, this Iowa farm boy had been exposed, firsthand, to the rigors of roughing it in the woods during frigid winter temperatures, sleeping on the snow-covered ground around a campfire in sleeping bags.

"That was quite an adventure," Marion chuckled as he found himself embroiled in fond reminiscences of those memorable weeks spent hunting, fishing and trapping in the survival-necessitated tradition of the Finnish natives.

"One night while we were sleeping, a spark from a birch log landed in my beard, which hadn't been shaved for quite a spell. My whiskers were on fire when I awakened and the next thing I knew, Edgar and a friend of his were swarming all over me tryin' to extinguish the blaze.

"The area up around Buck Lake is still quite primitive in lots of ways," Marion, whose natural gift as a narrator was serving all of us in good stead at the time, continued.

"On Saturday night, while I was up there that time, a bunch of fellows from the Buck Lake area were sort of whoopin' it up at the Inn—which serves as the community center for all the folks in that vicinity—when a group of young studs from Hibbing dropped in on us.

"If they were lookin' for trouble, they had come to the right place. Next thing you know, a gang fight was in full swing. One of our guys busted one of the trouble-seeking intruders in the jaw and the guy, half stunned, sort of stumbled back against the front-end of a Model A Ford parked nearby.

"Before he could get back on his feet, his opponent commenced stompin' the poor guy down into the space between the grille and the front bumper. It was quite a chore to get him out. The Hibbing bunch left for home soon after that and our folks continued with their tipplin' and visiting as though nothing had happened.

These Finns are no one to fool with, if you're lookin' for trouble, believe me."

Several other exciting episodes that had taken place during that adventurous outing served to whet my anticipation for the upcoming exposure to a lifestyle drastically in contrast to the more mundane "corn-hog" clime of central Iowa that was temporarily being left behind.

LET'S GO HUNTIN'

It was breaking daylight when we reached Grand Rapids. Negotiating our way through Minneapolis, now some 165 miles behind us, had proven relatively easy, due to the marked absence of heavy traffic at the time of night we had passed through that sizable metropolis.

Someone's suggestion that we make a pit-stop for breakfast, along with the need to visit a comfort station, met with unanimous approval.

"Grand Rapids is the county seat of Itasca County," Marion ventured between eager sips of fresh, steaming hot coffee. "We've got the major portion of the trip behind us. Lots of small towns between here and Nashwauk. We're in the Iron Range, now, y'know.

"Hibbing is further on up Highway 169 from Nashwauk. It has the largest open-pit iron ore mine in the entire world. We probably won't get a chance to see that today. The Brooks' live about 12 miles or so north of Nashwauk on Highway 65; just beyond Buck Lake a mile or two, at the most."

It was about 8 a.m. when our foursome passed the Buck Lake Inn, a sprawling, weathered, one-story log building situated only a short distance off the highway to our left. About a mile on up the road, the dense growth of trees on either side of the highway, suddenly gave way to an impressive view of the westernmost tip of the tranquil little lake on our right.

After passing the lake, the density of road-side trees and foliage continued once more, for what seemed a greater distance than it actually entailed. Then, on our left, a large clearing suddenly made its appearance. Back in from the gravel-surfaced highway some 100 yards, nestled the unpretentious buildings of the Brooks' farmstead, consisting of a sizable log house, a large hip-roofed barn and several smaller outbuildings.

"Well, we're here!" Betty chirped, as we turned in off the highway and made our way past an expanse of recently-planted garden just short of the house. "There doesn't seem to be anyone at home from the looks of things. I guess we really should have let them know that we were coming."

Her knock on the front door produced no response. Despite the hour's being relatively early, it was quite obvious that the family had departed the premises, perhaps to attend church services since it was Sunday, now, as well as a national holiday.

"Let's drive on back to Edgar and Allie's place. They're no doubt at home," she suggested as she climbed back into the car.

"There's a short-cut we could take by driving on ahead through that lane up ahead," Marion informed us, "but I think we'd have to open and close several gates. The lane goes through a pasture that Fred's cattle graze in. Maybe we had better go around by the road, instead."

We had been taking turns driving during the entire journey and Marion was at the wheel at the moment. Traveling only a short distance on up the highway, he turned westward onto a narrow, unimproved road that had been cut through a thick growth of aspen and evergreen to provide access to the smaller homestead, built shortly after Edgar and Allie had gotten married some five years prior.

When we had traveled westward some 60 rods or so, the road made a sharp turn to the left and crossed a little stream that lazily meandered its winding way across the Brooks' property from east to west. A rattling of heavy wood planking, cut from native timber, heralded our passage over the creek, acoustically amplified by the presence of dense underbrush roundabout.

A short distance beyond the bridge, a large clearing suddenly made its appearance. Nestled in a harmonious essence with its rustic surroundings, stood a medium-sized frame house, a small barn and several still smaller outbuildings, set apart from the meadowland beyond by a woven-wire fence that circumvented the buildings on every side. Once again, there was no response to Betty's knock on the door, save for the loud barking of a dog emanating from one of the outbuildings.

"Looks like we'll have to kill the day as best we can," Marion quipped. "Apparently, the whole family has taken off early for a celebration somewhere in the area. Anyone in favor of taking a short nap right here in the car?"

After our having gone more than 24 hours without sleep, his suggestion needed no urging to meet with unanimous approval. However, sleeping while sitting upright in an automobile hardly supplants sleeping in a comfortable bed, so our endeavor to get some much-needed rest was soon abandoned.

The day was spent driving here and there about the area, including a visit to the open-pit iron ore mine at Hibbing. It was late in the afternoon when we arrived back at the farm and, by coincidence, the Brooks clan returned from their day's outing at about the same time.

A mutually enjoyable round of greetings was engaged in for a time, after which the elder Mrs. Brooks insisted upon preparing supper for her unexpected guests, despite our expressed reluctance to impose upon her hospitality.

Edgar, Allie and little Marjorie took leave in order to attend to their evening chores, consisting of milking the cows, gathering the eggs and feeding a small herd of hogs.

"How would you folks like to go roller skating over to Hibbing later this evening?" Edgar inquired of us as they were preparing to depart for home. And with that brief suggestion, the unforeseen ensuing events to follow were set in motion.

Information to the affect that several fellows from the Buck Lake area were planning to go deer hunting after the skating party was over was somehow brought to the attention of Marion and myself. Moreover, we were asked by one of these men, who was acquainted with Edgar, if we would like to tag along. Despite the fact that our dire need for long overdue sleep had intensified greatly, we decided to accept the unexpected invitation. Few, if any, deer were existent in Iowa at that time and the prospects of merely seeing one, to say nothing of hunting one of these beautiful creatures, presented a challenge of no small dimension, to me at least.

It was nearing midnight when the headlights of an approaching auto heralded the arrival of the party Marion and I had made arrangements to accompany on a nocturnal deer hunting expedition. To our surprise, the driver was the sole occupant of the car, a roadster with the top folded down.

"Our friend couldn't make it," the fellow behind the wheel explained. "I'm going to drive over to my brother-in-law's place and see if he wants to go along. We can all sit here in the front seat for now, at least."

Turning down a narrow passageway leading into a heavily wooded area off of the highway, we bounced over an unimproved road for what seemed nearly a mile, but was probably less. The makeshift road came to a halt at a small clearing entirely surrounded by a dense growth of jack pines.

The beam of the headlights divulged a small frame shack nestled in the center of the cleared area. Driving to within only a few feet of the front door, our companion alighted and entered the small abode without bothering to knock. Obviously, the inhabitants were in bed asleep.

"Come on, get up, son; let's go deer huntin'," we could hear him addressing someone inside. Then a distinct thump could be heard by both of us sitting in the car outside. It turned out that our impetuous friend had turned back the covers at the foot of the bed where his sister and her husband were sleeping and grasping the unsuspecting fellow by both ankles, had literally yanked him out of bed. It was his butt striking the floor that had produced the aforementioned audible thump.

Almost quicker than it takes to tell it, the two men emerged through the doorway. The new addition to our entourage was cradling a shotgun in the crook of one arm while stuffing his shirttail into his trousers with the other. After a brief introduction, he climbed into the open rumble seat of the roadster and we started threading our way slowly back to the main road.

Several hours had been spent, after our arrival at the heavily wooded game reserve, traversing the labyrinth of logging trails that interlaced the posted area, when our driver brought the roadster to an abrupt halt.

"There's one back in there to our right," he whispered to our gun slinger seated behind him. Out of the corner of his eye, he had caught a glimpse of the telltale bright blue dots shining through the underbrush as the animal had curiously turned its head in the direction of our headlights.

Grasping his shotgun and flashlight, he slipped quietly from the rumble seat and commenced making his way stealthily into the dense growth of trees and bushes. I had followed him only a few steps, but had decided it best not to proceed farther, when the thunderous retort of the shotgun, somewhere up ahead, reverberated loudly through the forest all around us. An accompanying flash of fire from the barrel of the man's weapon marked his location and I started progressing toward him once more.

The night's silence was shattered by a violent crackling of brush followed by a second explosive retort from the shotgun. Aided in my passage through the undergrowth by the beam of his flashlight darting to and fro, I reached his side in a matter of seconds. When I drew alongside, the man was laughing raucously.

"It's a damned good thing I got him with my second shot," he announced. "That critter wasn't at all happy with me when I wounded him with the first one. About three more feet and he would have nailed me for sure. A wounded buck can be pretty mean and this fellow was no exception."

The full significance of his comment struck me with high impact as he directed the beam of his light upon the motionless carcass of a good-sized buck now lying at his predator's feet, where the angrily charging animal had finally fallen dead.

Together, we dragged the beautiful beast back to the car where it was draped over and firmly secured to the spare tire for our homeward journey.

In the heated tempo of this exciting adventure, little thought on my part had been given to the fact that what we had just now been up to was strictly illegal and subject to a fine of up to $1,000 if apprehended by a game warden.

"What would you do if you got caught?" I inquired somewhat meekly of the two natives.

"Well, let's see, now," the driver jested. "A deer like this one brings about $8 over in

Hibbing, if it's dressed out, etc. Folks over there are glad for the chance to buy fresh venison anytime they can get it."

The amazing fellow then proceeded to figure out in his head how many deer he would have to shoot, illegally, and sell for $8 a head to pay off the $1,000 fine!

Needless to say, I was immensely relieved to arrive home safely. By this time, Marion and I had been without the benefit of any sleep, to amount to anything, for nearly two days and two nights.

2

Buck Lake hospitality

Edgar had completed his morning chores and we were all seated at the breakfast table when he made the impromptu suggestion that we three men go fishing. Within the hour, the three of us, toting our fishing equipment, found ourselves making a mile-long trek on foot across a tundra-like valley that lay between the road and the inland lake for which we were headed.

I was commencing to wonder how much farther it was to our destination when, rounding a little knoll on the otherwise flat terrain, I received the answer to my pondering. Dead ahead, its breeze-initiated, rippled surface merrily reflecting the warm rays of the early morning sun, lay Grass Lake in silent but impressive splendor.

During our trek across the valley, I had speculated as to why the dearth of full-grown trees so vividly in evidence around us.

"This entire area was completely burned off some years back," Edgar volunteered. "Those little saplings springing up here and there are new growth just now reestablishing itself."

It was as though he had read my mind, so timely was his report concerning the forest fire that had swept through the area, turning everything in its path to ashes.

Partially obscured by a healthy overgrowth of tall reeds, an old wooden boat lay where it had been pulled up onto the bank and moored to a large rock by its anchor rope at some former time. Some 15 minutes were required to bale out an accumulation of water—some of it from ensuing spring rains and an equal amount from minute seepage through that portion of the boat's flat bottom that hadn't been pulled up onto dry land.

"Old Bessie will probably leak a little," Edgar quipped as the three of us prepared to shove off from shore. "Haven't had occasion to use it for quite a spell. Allie and I built this old scow by ourselves a few years back. We packed the material in on foot and assembled it right here. It was well into late evening by the time we had finished puttin' it together. Allie had to hold the flashlight so I could drive the last of the nails in."

Rowing away from shore a 100 yards or so, Edgar tossed out the anchor and began casting a red and white Daredevil spoon. He recommended Marion and I use the same. On his third cast, I saw his pole suddenly bow nearly double and heard the high pitched squeal of his reel as the northern he had just hooked streaked away in a desperate struggle to free itself from the treble hook now firmly attached to its upper jaw.

"Got a good one on," our host shouted, "but I'm gonna have to start turning him around pretty quick; he's takin' out a lot of my line."

I had made perhaps six or seven casts when a northern hit my lure with such force that the pole was nearly wrenched from my grip. The strike had caught me a little off guard as I had been devoting some of my attention to watching Edgar skillfully play his catch. Up to this time, my experience at fishing had been limited to catching small bullheads or bluegills using a simple cane pole with a worm on the hook and a cork bobber to tell me when I had a bite. This was a different ball game!

"I've got one, too!" I bellowed, and started cranking on my casting reel. In my excitement, my fingers lost contact with the resisting handles several times as they commenced whirling backwards with a high-pitched singing sound.

"Thumbing" the rapidly unwinding reel, I soon succeeded in slowing up the desperate run for freedom my hooked fish was making. Eventually, and with a sigh of relief, I seemed to have it responding to my resumed cranking and it was headed toward the boat.

Following the welcome advice of my two companions, I was giving my fish plenty of time to tire itself a bit when Edgar lifted his catch into the boat. It was the largest fish that I had ever seen.

"Guess he'll go about nine pounds, maybe 10," the veteran sportsman grunted matter-of-factly. But to me, the sight of that 30 inch beauty, with the sun's rays coruscating on its silver and gray scales as Edgar held it up for our inspection, was a sight conducive to a feeling of mild ecstasy.

It appeared that I was about to land my fish when it suddenly took off in a power dive for the bottom of the lake. Before I knew it, things were right back to about where we had started.

"I think you might be able to handle him better if you can come back here where I'm sittin'," Edgar suggested. "We'll just reverse our positions." We carefully traded places in the boat and in due time, I succeeded in boating my first northern ever.

"Speakin' of reversing positions reminds me of a story I heard awhile back," Edgar addressed Marion and me without any noticeable interruption in his continued casting. "There was this woodsman who had died; had a fatal accident while felling a tall jack pine out in the forest. The pallbearers at his funeral consisted of six big strapping lumberjacks. When it came time to carry the casket from the church out to the hearse, the undertaker happened to notice, just as they were about to place it in the shiny black vehicle, that the coffin was headed the wrong way.

"'Hold up there, reverse the corpse, please,' the mortician directed the pallbearers. The big fellows just stood there, obviously failing to comprehend just exactly what the undertaker was instructing them to do. By this time, the crowd was swarming out of the church in large numbers.

"'Reverse the corpse, I say!' the mortician thundered, impatiently. Again no response.

"'Maybe you had better let me handle this,' one of the pallbearers, who happened to be the foreman of the lumber camp, interjected. Then, in a loud, authoritative voice, he shouted the command, 'End for end the bastard!'

"Whereupon, the pallbearers immediately proceeded to oblige the astonished undertaker's wishes. They reversed the coffin in order for the corpse's head to enter the hearse first, instead of its feet, and gently slid it into its proper place."

Despite Edgar's story having struck me funny, to the point of laughing aloud as I reeled my by now tiring fish up close to the side of the boat, I finally succeeded in landing it without mishap. To this day, more than 50 years later, I am reminded of that story whenever I observe a casket being placed in a hearse.

Edgar's earlier speculation that the fishing might be pretty good that day turned out to be correct. An enviable catch of nice northerns adorned our stringers when we arrived back at Edgar and Allie's place along about the middle of the afternoon.

Marion and I, feeling like a couple of zombies by this time, managed to stay awake just long enough to help clean the fish. Then we sought out a shady spot beneath a tree in the house yard and after removing our shoes, stretched ourselves out on the grass and immediately fell asleep. But not for long!

Betty and Jo, now adequately rested by reason of having gotten a good night's sleep during our nocturnal escapade up in the game reserve deer hunting, began tickling the bottoms of our feet with some leaf-tipped branches they had plucked from our shade tree.

Highly amused at our frustrated and unsolicited arousal from a sound slumber, those two Iowa gals never realized just how closely they had come to being victims of homicide, especially following their third or fourth insistence upon disturbing our cherished nap time.

In our state of semi-hallucination, we might

well have strangled the both of them without encountering undue feelings of remorse for having instinctively retaliated to their deviltry. Eventually, they opted for allowing us to resume our desperately-needed rest without further disturbance.

Marion and I were aroused from our sound sleep by the gentle nudging of the toe of one of Edgar's boots against our ribs.

"The women folks say it's time to eat supper," comprised his mildly apologetic summons.

Meandering in sleep-drugged stupor over to the pump in the yard, the two of us dashed cold water on our faces before entering the house.

When all of us were seated, Allie placed a large kettle of steaming hot chowder on the dining table within easy reach of each one of us and after adding a platter piled high with oven-warmed homemade bread and an ample supply of butter to go with it, indicated with a slight nod of her head that each of us was to ladle our own helping at will.

I had partaken of only a few spoonfuls of the tasty delicacy when I knew it was something special. "I don't know exactly what it is," I quipped, "but it's the best tasting dish of its kind I've ever eaten. How is it made?"

"It's called Kalamojakka," Allie informed us. "It's easy to make. Cut up the potatoes and the onions into small cubes and boil them in water until they are very near completely cooked. Then, drop in the small chunks of filleted fish, which require only a few minutes—four minutes, or so—season it to your liking, add the milk and serve it hot."

"You're eating the northern pike we caught today," Edgar informed us. "Northerns have some bones in the filets, so be a little careful you don't get one of them in your throat."

It was a meal I've never forgotten, even now after the passage of more than 50 years. I guess I've eaten just about every kind of chowder to be sought after anywhere, but this preparation had that little "extra something" that set it apart from all the others.

Allie was Finn, I knew, and Kalamojakka was definitely a Finnish term. Hence, I concluded, and rightly so, I'm sure, that it was some special Finnish touch that made the difference.

The balance of that Monday evening was spent visiting a bit. Perhaps some of the folks from the big house might have dropped over, also. I don't rightly recall.

The following two days provided us with the time and opportunity to become better acquainted with other members of the Brooks clan— Thelma, Edgar's older sister, who lived with her husband on a small farm nearby; George, an older brother, employed by the State Highway Commission at the time; and Buddy (Fred Jr.), a teenage brother still living at home with his parents.

The evening that we spent visiting George and his family was especially enhanced by his performance of numerous slight-of-hand tricks with a deck of playing cards.

We learned later that when George was just a youngster back in Iowa, Fred had hired a card shark he knew to teach his eldest son "everything there was to know about handling a deck of cards." After watching his deft fingers do things with those playing cards that bordered on incredulity, it was obvious he had learned his lessons well.

"Did you ever have any occasion to use your skill in dealing cards while playing poker for money?" I ventured to ask of George after he had dealt me a royal flush from a seemingly well-shuffled deck.

"Only once," he replied with a wry little smile. "I used to own a logging truck when I was younger. The rear end went out of it down around Duluth and I lacked enough pocket money with which to have it repaired.

"I got wind of a high-stakes poker game goin' on in the back room of a tavern in the town where I was stranded and invited myself to sit in on it. When I had won the 50 bucks I needed to get my truck fixed, I left the game. I've never played poker for money since."

During our visit with the Brooks family, we were impressed by the fact that, even now in July, they had ice readily available for keeping food refrigerated in their iceboxes.

This was accomplished by stacking up a large supply of cubed cakes of ice cut from the frozen surface of a nearby lake during the winter and covering the pile with a protective layer of sawdust from the sawmill. The insulation, so provided, prevented the stored ice from thawing out all through the warmer months of summer.

Filleted fish were kept from spoiling for extended periods of time by packing them along with pure salt in wooden barrels. Produce from their gardens was canned in large volume, assuring them of an adequate supply of wholesome vegetables the year 'round.

It was self-evident that these refugees from the big depression in Iowa were now faring very nicely; and doing it with a minimum of stress and physical exertion, in contrast with the faster pace they had once felt to be necessary for survival.

By the time Thursday morning rolled around,

we were readying our affairs for the homeward journey back to Iowa. I had become thoroughly enchanted with northern Minnesota; totally hooked, in a manner of speaking, on the lifestyle of these good people, compared to the more stringent schedule required of me to make a decent living back home.

"How were things up here during the depression?" I inquired of Edgar as we were packing our things into the car on the morning of our departure. Vividly recalling the deprivation of creature comforts that infamous collapse of the nation's economy had subjected my immediate family to, it seemed a moot question on my part. By reason of my father's having undergone extended periods of unemployment after our large family had left the farm and moved to the city, we had learned all too well the essence of poverty.

"Was there a depression?" Edgar answered with tongue in cheek. "We just lived the same way folks up this way had always lived—plenty of fish and wild game for meat the year around, milked a few cows, raised a good garden, burned wood for heat, canned lots of vegetables to carry us through the winter. It's a simple life, but it's a good life. Not too many folks around here suffering from ulcers from bein' uptight all the time." And there was nothing about his forthright depiction of their lifestyle to indicate otherwise.

BACK TO REALITY

"Well, what did you think of all this?" Marion queried of me when we had gotten underway.

"It's been a fantastic outing," I responded, "and I'm afraid if we had stayed up here much longer, I would have given thought to calling

25

home and telling the folks to dispose of our household goods and close up the house because we had decided to stay up here in the Buck Lake area indefinitely."

"I know what you mean," Marion acquiesced. "I felt the same way the first time I came up into this country."

As we journeyed southward, Marion shared with us some additional episodes of interest that had occurred during his all-winter sojourn with the Brooks family early in his and Betty's marriage. An interesting conversationalist in his own right, his outflow of words provided a pleasant dimension of adventure to what might otherwise have been merely a monotonous passage of miles.

Inevitably, our conversation soon turned to the subject of the illicit hunting of deer out of season—a practice that for as long as anyone could remember, had apparently prevailed amongst the natives of the region we had just left behind us.

"If you want to eat fresh meat, you hunt," was an adage that had been handed down from generation to generation.

"I was getting quite apprehensive last Sunday night when I became aware that we were driving within a few rods of the game warden's home with that buck draped over our spare tire in plain sight," I reminisced.

"It's risky business, to be sure," Marion affirmed. "The conservation officers know full well what's goin' on and, of course, they have a job to do; everyone understands that. But they have learned the hard way, over a long period of time, that there is a limit to how hard they can crack down on these Finns, who sort of figure they were here and doing their thing long before these game hunting laws were established."

"Legend has it that, back in the early days, a couple of game wardens who had been assigned to the Buck Lake area got to throwing their weight around a bit much. They simply disappeared, all of a sudden," Marion continued. "Whether they just packed up and left, or whether they wound up in the bottom of a lake somewhere, was a matter of speculation. In due time, some sort of truce has been established between the law and the local folks, I guess.

"I heard tell of this native who got cornered by the law one night up in that same area we were hunting Sunday night. They had him dead to rights, they figured.

"Well, this fellow bailed out of the car with his rifle and flashlight and instructed his wife, who had been driving their auto, to give the lawman a merry chase over them loggin' roads long enough for him to make his way across 11 miles of bogs and thorn-infested thicket to the sanctuary of their home. I guess he set a new record for cross-country runnin' that night!

"He had barely gotten back home and out of what was left of his thorn-shredded clothing when the game wardens, with his wife in custody, drove up to the house. Feigning that he had been awakened from a sound sleep, this moonlighting deer hunter made his appearance in the doorway, yawning and stretching, demanding of these unwelcome intruders as to, 'Just what the hell's goin' on here?'"

"He got away with it; bluffed his way out of a close scrape that could have proven costly. I suppose it placed his wife in somewhat of a compromising situation, but there's no law against a woman taking a car ride in the woods late at night, y'know.

"The law tried to catch that fellow red-handed for years, but never quite succeeded in doing so. They knew he was poachin' deer regularly, but he always managed to outwit them," Marion concluded.

We arrived back in Wright County without any adverse mishaps en route and melted back into the groove of our respective lifestyles in short order—Marion with his farming operation and I back on my route as a successful Fuller Brush man.

I was 20 years of age when that memorable trip up to Buck Lake occurred. The year was 1940, and a fellow by the name of Adolph Hitler was commencing to create havoc throughout central Europe. Pearl Harbor, that "Day of Infamy," in the words of then president Franklin D. Roosevelt, lay only 18 months ahead in world history.

3

Bright idea

Twenty-two years passed. Not until the summer of 1962 did we have occasion to renew our acquaintance with Edgar and Allie.

During a trip across the entire expanse of northern Minnesota, from west to east, my wife and I decided to make inquiry in the Buck Lake vicinity as to the whereabouts of our friends. From relatives, we learned that Edgar and Allie and their daughter, Marjorie, were currently engaged in the operation of a thriving taxidermy business in Minneapolis.

We continued on to Ely and on down Highway Number One to the Silver Bay and Two Harbors region before heading back toward Iowa in earnest. I had become interested in two newly-built rail lines extending from Lake Superior inland to the heart of the Iron Range country.

A recently-developed procedure for processing iron ore into refined pellets, called Taconite, had literally revolutionized the iron ore mining industry. The two new rail lines had been built to expedite the transporting of iron ore from the inland mines to Silver Bay and Two Harbors, to be loaded onto ocean-going ships for overseas destinations as well as to steel mills in the eastern area of the United States.

By this time, I had been a locomotive engineer for more than 20 years on the Illinois Central Railroad. If I could hire on running an engine for either of these lines during the summer months, I reasoned, I could get in some good fishing at the same time. As it turned out, my idea didn't reach fruition. My employer didn't see fit to grant me the requested leave-of-absence that I needed to accomplish this objective.

Our itinerary back to Waterloo, Iowa, where we now lived, called for our traveling through Minneapolis. Locating Brooks' Taxidermy Service entailed little difficulty. As it was only a relatively short distance off of our route, we decided to pay Edgar and Allie at least a brief visit. At that time, they were conducting their business in the basement of their nice home in a residential section of northeast Minneapolis.

It was self-evident, upon our arrival, that the huge volume of patronage from sportsmen seeking their expertise in the mounting of wild game trophies left them precious little time to engage in socializing. However, during our short time with them, we were graciously provided with a comprehensive tour of their fascinating operation, during which time I snapped some colored pictures with my 35mm Zeiss Contaflex. These snapshots are still a part of my many albums of photos taken in almost every section of the United States.

We engaged in a friendly exchange of chit-chat while partaking of several cups of hot coffee and some tasty cookies that Marjorie had set out during our excursion through the assembly-line procedure. Then, after cordial parting gestures, we were soon on our way once again.

Although we indirectly received word concerning Edgar and Allie by way of relatives, it was to be 29 years before the occasion to see them again would present itself. This occurred during a visit in August of 1991 with friends from Iowa who were spending some time at their summer home at Mille Lacs Lake, Minnesota.

A sight-seeing trip on up into the Hibbing area found its way into our agenda one day. A brief stop-over was made at the large Wal-Mart Store in Grand Rapids and while the rest of our party was engaged in shopping, I perused the telephone directory in a pay phone booth, hoping to find Edgar and Allie listed therein. My quest proved successful and within a matter of seconds after making the call, Edgar's voice came booming over the line.

Arrangements were quickly made for a brief stop-over on the part of our small group at their place of residence. Instructions as to how to get there were scribbled on a piece of scrap paper, and after succeeding in corralling the rest of the gang from scattered areas of the large market-place, we were soon headed on up Highway 169 in a northeasterly direction.

The names Coleraine, Bovey, Marble and Pengilly, all small hamlets lying between Grand Rapids and Nashwauk, struck chords of nostalgia in the archives of my memory as we passed through them. For the most part, I could detect little in the way of any drastic changes they had undergone over the passage of years since we had last driven this route.

It was nearing 11:30 a.m. when we pulled into the driveway and onto the blacktopped parking area adjacent to a lovely, modern, frame dwelling situated on the north shore of Buck Lake and only several rods off the main highway. As I awaited a response to my knock on the door, I found myself pondering what changes in their physical appearance would inevitably have taken place since seeing them last.

Edgar answered my summons, his broad shoulders nearly filling the doorway; a bit heavier than I remembered him to be and, like myself, baldish of pate. His firm handshake attested to the strength that was still existent in arms and big hands that had put hundreds of hours on one end of a cross-cut saw while felling timber back in the old days, long past.

Following our host through the kitchen area of the tastefully furnished home, we came upon the lady of the house seated in a Kennedy rocking chair in the living room. Directly above her, a beautiful moose head, mounted on a walnut wall plaque, gazed out with life-like essence at the new arrivals into the large carpeted room.

Extending an outstretched paw, as I approached the smiling person seated in the rocker, I exclaimed boldly, "Allie Peratalo Brooks!"

The expression of surprise that appeared on her face at this unanticipated salutation, bespoke her amazement over someone she hardly remembered, in the passage of so many years, having called her by her full name. What she had failed to take into account was the fact that, despite the limitations of its existence during all this time, their acquaintanceship had held a special ranking of high priority in any listing of people we had come to know during the course of our lifetime.

"Have you folks had lunch?" I promptly inquired. "If not, may I suggest that we drive down to the Buck Lake Inn for some vittles." I had noticed the restaurant sign on the building when we had driven past it a few minutes earlier.

I was informed that our hosts of the moment didn't ordinarily partake of midday meals to any extent, but that an exception might be in order under the circumstances. Then Edgar made the suggestion that he show us around the place a bit before we went to eat.

An interesting aspect of their present lifestyle pleasantly surprised our entire party during the tour of the house. It was divulged that, after retiring from the taxidermy business a number of years prior, this couple had put together a two-piece, husband-and-wife team called Edgar & Allie's Coo-Coo-Band.

With Edgar on the drums, Allie with her tambourine, and both singing to the accompaniment of taped background music, produced by Edgar's brother, Fred, and Fred's wife, June, the two of them frequently put on musical performances to entertain residents of care centers throughout their area, and at festivals of sorts, as well. This despite the fact of Allie's having undergone serious surgery on her spine only a relatively short time prior, for a condition that had plagued her for many years.

At Edgar's suggestion, we were directed to a finished-off room in the basement, where a professional ensemble of drums of all descriptions was observable at one end of the walk-out room.

Donning western style hats and taking their respective positions behind the musical instruments, the acoustical-oriented room was soon

33

reverberating with the couple's gusty rendition of "The Pennsylvania Polka," followed by the pleasing strains of "The Green, Green Grass of Home."

It took little in the way of imagination to relate to the reasons for their obvious popularity throughout the Iron Range country. We learned too, while there, that Edgar had been an active participant in the Alcoholics Anonymous rehabilitation program for eight or nine years; and, as a matter of fact, was scheduled to give a talk at a hospital in the area that very night. Little wonder that my fascination with what I was discovering about this couple, whom we had first met under drastically different circumstances, was uncovering new horizons with each passing moment!

We had gone back upstairs and were preparing to leave the house when my attention was directed to a thick, ring-binder scrapbook that was lying at random on the large antique oak dining table. Taking advantage of the fact that the women folks were tarrying a bit in our intended departure, I took it upon myself to thumb through its voluminous contents.

Noting my interest in the scrapbook data, Edgar briefed me, comprehensively, on the highlights of its depictions, not only of their intriguing years in the taxidermy business, but of their more recent involvement in the musical entertainment enterprise.

"To borrow a popular phrase used by a well-known tobacco company, 'You've come a long way, Baby'," I said to Edgar, as we closed the delightful scrapbook. As I was perusing page upon page of its contents, I had sensed myself being swept up into an aura of enthrallment and profound respect for their accomplishments, not the least of which was their current endeavor to bring a commendable dimension of joy into the preponderantly mundane lifestyle in which many senior citizens find themselves entrapped.

"I think I would like to write a biography of you two," I blurted out somewhat impetuously. "Now, I'm not exactly an Ernest Hemingway or a Thomas Wolfe, as far as being an author is concerned; but I have put a few million words down on paper during the past 40 years, and I believe I could put something together that you might like in the way of a tribute to what you have done and are now doing with your lives." Then the matter was dropped as our small group, including Edgar and Allie, filed out the door.

Lack of extra room in our automobile made it necessary for us to take two cars to the combination tavern and restaurant a mile or so to the south. As we entered the unpretentious, one-story, weathered log building, it was obvious that Edgar and Allie were well-known and highly respected by everyone seated at the long bar that we circumvented on our way to the spacious dining area beyond.

Our orders were taken and, while waiting for our food to be prepared and brought out, I engaged myself in some reminiscences that went way back to our first trip to Buck Lake more than 50 years prior. Within only a matter of minutes, an atmosphere of cordial rapport had completely swept aside any tendencies of inhibition that may have been mildly in evidence a bit earlier.

Edgar smiled and chuckled softly when I called to mind his old story about "end-for-ending the bastard." Then, true to the tradition that I remembered so well, he sprung a new one on those of us seated at the table:

"Do any of you know why Johnny Cash sang

the song 'Ring of Fire?' He got his Ben-Gay mixed up with his Preparation H."

A titter of amusement was evoked by his joke and about that time, as though acting on cue, the waitress made her appearance from the kitchen pushing a portable serving table piled high with our food.

Subsequent to leaving the house and during the course of the meal at the Inn, nothing more had been mentioned concerning my earlier idea about writing the biography. But as our little group started making preparations to get into our automobile after lunch, Edgar reintroduced the subject.

"What would you need in the way of material in order to write that book?" he inquired out of the blue.

"Well, just about anything and everything you might be able to muster together in the way of pertinent information and data of sorts, going back to the time you were born," I replied.

"I'll see what I can drum up for you. You'll be hearing from us."

It was obvious that this old-timer from Buck Lake was warming up to my idea with growing enthusiasm. Then, after a cordial round of farewells and warm handshakes, we were on our way once more to pursue the remainder of the day's itinerary.

THE STORY UNFOLDS

Several weeks after our return to our summer home in beautiful northeast Iowa, we concluded a pending sale of our property overlooking the main channel of the Mississippi River. Early in October, our winter home in

Brownsville, Texas became our full-time residence.

Several weeks after our final migration to the Rio Grande Valley, a rather sizable box was delivered to our house by United Parcel Service. Its contents consisted of the scrapbook I had perused at Buck Lake nearly two months prior, along with four audio tape cassettes Edgar had made, depicting the highlights of his entire lifetime from early on to the present.

Without the time restriction that had limited my initial viewing of the scrapbook, an even deeper sense of enthrallment with its contents developed at each turn of a new page. Memorabilia carried me, as though being transported on a magic flying carpet, through an overview of Edgar and Allie's life covering a span of more than half of a century together.

There were pictures of their early days on the farm only a short distance from Buck Lake and some taken during their operation of the resort on Napoleon Lake a bit later; also pictures and copies of newspaper articles and clippings from well-known sports magazines, covering their 27 years in the taxidermy business. It was all there in vivid detail.

While visiting our Iowa friends at Lake Mille Lacs during the prior August, I had noticed a huge muskie or northern fish mounted on a walnut plaque and hanging on the wall above the fireplace mantle in the spacious clubhouse of the Sherwood Forest Resort. I wasn't particularly surprised to note that the polished brass badge plate in the lower corner of the plaque was labeled, "Brooks Taxidermy Service, Minneapolis, Minnesota." As a matter-of-fact, this discovery had been the catalyst that had triggered my desire to make contact with Edgar and Allie once again after the passage of nearly 30 years since having seen them last.

Particularly impressive, as I continued to peruse the scrapbook, were the listings and in some instances, photos of well-known public figures who had seen fit to bring their wild game and fowl trophies to Brooks Taxidermy by reason of the latter having earned a reputation for excellent workmanship. Included in these names were presidents and vice presidents of the United States, the governors of several states and a well-known professional football coach, to designate only a few.

My attention then moved to newspaper articles and personal letters of acknowledgement incidental to entertainment programs in which Edgar and Allie's Coo-Coo Band had participated during more recent years following their retirement from the taxidermy business. Pages were filled with clippings depicting Edgar and Allie alongside well-known figures in the musical world, including a former pianist with Lawrence Welk's Band. In another instance, a syndicated newspaper columnist of world renown was featured on the same program as the Coo-Coo Band.

Again, as had been the case in my earlier viewing of this correlation of memorabilia, communiques from numerous nursing homes and senior citizen organizations throughout the Iron Range commandeered my profound respect for this remarkable couple. For the most part, these letters were expressions of appreciation and gratitude for Edgar and Allie's having participated in social programs that had been indisputably enhanced by the quaint vibrancy of their musical presentations.

Moving on to the tapes narrated by Edgar, personally, I found myself becoming more deeply immersed in an aura of rapport with his earthy portrayal of his life history. His place of birth was only a short distance from the community in which my wife and I had spent our childhood days. Mild sensations of nostalgia accompanied my hearing familiar names, places and events out of the past as I edited the tape recordings.

Allie's handwritten epitome of her own life, which I had requested of her earlier, arrived in the mail about the time I had finished listening to Edgar's tapes.

Again, I found myself able to relate readily to her lifestyle during childhood days. Coming up the "hard way," without the benefits of many luxuries that have come to be taken for granted, even demanded, by the less affluent in today's society, had been my own lot in my younger years.

By this time, the enormity of the commitment I had made, during a moment of impetuosity, was commencing to make its presence known in the fullness of its reality. What to include and what to exclude, in all the data to be considered in the composition of this biography, has presented no small challenge in endeavoring to arrive at such decisions.

After carefully weighing the pros and cons of the matter in the balance, I have forsaken my original intent to paraphrase the contents of Edgar's tapes. Instead, I have undertaken the task of transcribing his recorded narration with little, if any, omissions.

I wish it were possible for each and every one of you, who will be, or are now reading *Back To Buck Lake* to be able to listen to these tapes as I have had the opportunity to do. Regretfully, this is an impossibility that is unavoidable, one which represents a definite loss in the overall essence of the story, for Edgar is a gifted and mirthful storyteller in his own right.

Authoring this, my first endeavor of its kind, has involved many hours of sometimes frustrating dedication to what I feel to have been a profoundly worthy undertaking on my part.

As the work progresses, I am frequently made aware that the forces, commencing with our first acquaintance with Edgar and Allie more than half a century ago and culminating in the publication of this book, represent a paradox of no small dimension. Truly, it has been said, "The Lord works in mysterious ways, His purposes to attain."

Edgar and Allie's extroversion, manifested so vividly by the social input of their Coo-Coo Band activities, is commendable. This attitude was the principle factor in providing the catalyst for setting in motion the writing of this book. Their musical program is proving itself a veritable vessel through which an emerald message is being conveyed—a message proclaiming that loving one's neighbor is the elixir for helping solve the ills of the world roundabout us.

The attitude of "me first, others later, should there chance to be any leftovers," is one that is all too prevalent wherever one looks. Replacing this attitude with one of genuine concern for the well-being of others, as well as self, is a quest that mankind stands sorely in need of. Such concern for those less fortunate than we, and endeavoring to do something about it, is my own private definition and interpretation of that evasive term we call love.

Edgar's Story

EDGAR BROOKS

4

Where there's trouble

(Transcribed from audio tape recordings provided by Edgar Brooks)

Hi folks! I'm Edgar Brooks, that good lookin' guy from up to Buck Lake. I'm going to attempt to come up with some sort of a biography of my life; and, believe me, that isn't going to be easy.

I was born in Rowan, Iowa, on January 9, 1916, so you can see that I'm no spring chicken.

Now, at this time, my parents were in the entertainment business in the state of Iowa. My dad was reasonably wealthy at the time. He had

43

several entertainment houses, a couple of grain elevators and several farms in the vicinity of Rowan. He also owned some houses and two grocery stores, one in Galt, Iowa, and the other one in Rowan. In addition to all this, were two movie theaters, one in Dows, Iowa, and the other one in Rowan, a dance hall and a roller skating rink.

They were doing quite well and managing all of these diverse enterprises was a stressful undertaking much of the time. This was the type of environment I was brought up in; a situation that was to undergo drastic change a few years on down the road.

Now the first little thing I remember happening was somewhat unusual, so I'll sort of get the ball rolling by sharing this particular episode with you:

DISAPPEARING ACT

My mother and father took me to a church supper one night when I was a small lad. I sat at one end of a big long table and there was this lady sitting down on the other end. This lady must have had Saint Vitus' Dance or some similar infirmity, for she was makin' all kinds of funny faces that caught my attention.

I looked up and saw her and I thought she was havin' fun with me, y'know. So I started making faces, too. Back and forth we went, she and I, makin' these faces. And the longer it went on, the worse she got. Of course, the worse she got, the worse I got. Oh boy! Was we cuttin' a rug, there!

I happened to look up at my mother along about then and the expression on her face had taken on the dimension of a thunderstorm brewing. Unbeknownst to me, she had been observing this performance and was highly displeased with it. By the look on her face, I knew I was doing something I wasn't supposed to be doing.

So, I thought the best thing for me to do might well be to simply disappear for awhile. That was a characteristic of mine when things got a little rough from time to time—I'd always do a disappearing act. I got myself away from the table and walked outside. When I got out there, I met a couple of boys I knew who were about my own age.

Across the street from the church was an apple orchard that belonged to the butcher there in Rowan—man by the name of Louie Stevenson.

We went over across the road to this orchard, crawled over the fence, and thought we would steal a few apples. That would be exciting, y'know. So we got up in the trees and about the time we got up in those trees, I saw a flashlight comin' down the sidewalk. I had a good idea that it might be the Justice of the Peace, Joe Patton. Buddy, did I get down out of that tree and take off! He saw me makin' tracks outa' there and took out after me.

I came to a culvert under the road and dived into it, but I didn't pull my feet in far enough. When he came along, I could see his light shining on my feet, but I didn't dare pull them in; didn't dare make a move.

So when he got there, he got me by the leg and pulled me back out of that culvert. Of course, he knew who I was, so he took me downtown to the bank. It wasn't very far, a couple of blocks at the most. He put me in that bank in a dark room and went out, locking up the bank behind him. I'll tell you, he scared me

45

damned near to death. I plain didn't know just what I was going to do.

What he did was go back to the church and get my dad and the two of them came on back to the bank. I don't remember what all they said, but I know I got quite a lecture. I decided, then and there, that I wasn't going to let that sort of thing happen again.

BIG SHOT

When I commenced to grow a bit older—old enough to get my eyes open and start to move around more, in a manner of speaking—I began to feel that I was gettin' to be quite a big shot. I thought people should look up to me.

My dad would give me coins from time to time—pennies, nickels, dimes, even quarters—sometimes quite a goodly bunch of them. Occasionally, I would stand on the sidewalk in front of our theater and toss those coins into the dust on the dirt street and watch the kids dig for them.

Now this seemed to do something for my ego. I don't know just what it was, but it gave me a feeling of superiority. At this time, I was probably six or seven years old, so you can see that I was gettin' off to a pretty good start. I was developing quite an opinion of myself, even at that early age.

HAIR-RAISING PICTURE SHOW

Now, there was another little episode that took place in my dad's theater in Rowan that my wife likes me to tell about:

In this theater was a double balcony with stairs going up to it from the ground floor at

both ends. At the bottom of each of these stair-
ways was a post. I used to stand on the lower
steps of the stairs behind these posts and watch
the shows. If I wouldn't have stood on the stairs,
I wouldn't have been able to see the screen at
the front of the theater.

On this particular night, there was a special
show on that I didn't want to miss. There was a
motorcycle rider and a couple of women in it. I
can even remember the name of that show:
"Hurricane Hutch." He was a motorcycle rider
who went through all sorts of shenanigans. Boy,
his act would get real exciting at times, at least
in my young mind.

I was standin' behind this post, watching the
show and I had some string in my hand. I don't
recall exactly why, but I had it. Now, I was
watchin' this show and things were gettin' real
exciting, when the dray man walked in and
leaned up against the other side of this post—
man by the name of Dan Fletcher, a very good
customer of dad's at the theater.

Dan's head came just about even with the
top of the post and about this time I was playin'
with this string, workin' it through my fingers.
Well, things were gettin' so exciting up there on
that movie screen, I couldn't hardly stand it;
and somehow, that string and my fingers got
tangled up in his hair.

About then, one of those motorcycles hit a
tree, ker-bang! I gave a jerk about then and out
came a bunch of Dan's hair! I guess I don't have
to tell you, Dad lost one of his very best customers at the theater, and I kinda' think I lost a
little prestige with this gentleman, too.

Boy, I'll tell you, if there was any way to get
into trouble back in those days, I'd find it.

47

THE SNOWBALL EPISODE

Now there was another little episode—boy, I can remember lots of episodes that I got into in this little town of Rowan! My dad's grain elevator was possibly four blocks from where we lived. You had to go past the hotel. Then, when you came to Main Street, which was only about two blocks long, it was only one more block beyond that to our place.

Along this street, there were benches and people would come to town on Saturday night and sit on these benches and visit. One of the regular occupants of one of these benches was my Uncle Frank. Uncle Frank had a habit of taking off his hat and scratching his head ever so often while he was talking to someone.

Well, I got to watchin' my uncle doing this one time, sittin' right there in front of the drug-store. Now this was in the wintertime and we had recently had a heavy snowfall.

So I got to watchin' this group of guys visiting and Uncle Frank scratching his head every few minutes, and I got to wondering if it wouldn't be sort of fun to get up on the roof of that drug store building, which had a ladder going up each side of it. Once up there, I could make me a big snowball from the snow on the flat roof and when Uncle Frank took his hat off to scratch his head, I'd crack him on top of the head with it. Seemed to me that would be kind of exciting.

So I did just that. I climbed up on top of the building and made me a nice big snowball packed good and firm and watched for Uncle Frank to take his hat off the next time. I didn't have to wait very long for him to do this and when he did, I let go with the big snowball and conked him right on top of the head!

Let me tell you, my uncle let out a roar that sounded like a wounded grizzly. He knew all too well just where that snowball had come from and he took off for the ladder on that side of the building. It sounded to me like Uncle Frank might have come from some sort of coastal state at some time in his life, maybe California or Florida, 'cause just about the time he got to the top of that ladder, I could hear him muttering something about "that little sun on the beach!"

Well, let me tell you this; by the time Uncle Frank got to the top of that building, that little feller on the roof was movin' for real! Hell, I'd already scrambled down the opposite ladder and was streakin' for home.

This Uncle Frank of mine had a reputation for bein' a little bit on the owlish and ornery side, at best, so I had little inclination to want to hang around to see what was going to happen. I wasn't sure if he would suspect who had blasted him with that snowball, but I suspected that he might have a pretty good idea who had done this to him; so I figured it might be a good idea to disappear for awhile. I was gettin' good at doin' that when I'd get into some sort of jam, which seemed to be occurring frequently in those days.

PONY AND CART

Now, as I began to grow a little older, my desires began to undergo some changes in nature. I found myself gettin' a kick out of a new adventure that popped into my head somewhere along the line. I commenced walking around where the cars were parked behind my dad's dance hall at night, shining my flashlight around and under them out of curiosity. While so doing, I began to notice that some of them

49

had shiny bottles of something stashed out of sight behind the back wheels.

Now, this was back in prohibition times. People couldn't take their bottles inside in those days. They would take a couple of snorts before going into the dance hall and hide the bottle under the wheel until they felt the desire to come back out, off and on during the evening, for another swig.

So I got to sampling the contents of some of those bottles when I'd come across one. Now, I had to be a little careful with this as most of this was 180 or 190 proof alcohol. One good shot of this would blow the top of your head off, so I got to looking for a bottle that had been spiked with near beer instead of tackling it straight.

When I found one I thought I could handle, I would take two or three snorts of it. Then, I would take some Sen-Sens so my folks wouldn't smell anything suspicious on my breath, and back into that dance hall I'd go, equal to anybody in there. I had found something for boosting my ego that I had never, never experienced before and it was really exciting!

Now, y'know, I could talk with anybody in there; I was as big as anyone in there; I was as important as everyone else in there. I wanted to be like the big boys and I had found the potion that really did the trick.

When I started sneakin' those first few sips, I never thought that there was an inherent chance of my becoming an alcoholic somewhere on down the line. I didn't even know what that term meant. In those days, a man who drank too much booze was termed a "drunkard." Back then, it wasn't called a disease; it was adjudged to be a serious flaw in one's character.

I'm not real sure that I ever did become a genuine, 14 carat alcoholic, but I'll tell you right now, if I didn't, I came real close to it. Y'know, I always thought imbibing in liquor was like a light bulb—that, if you wanted it, you turned it on, and when you didn't want any more, you simply turned it off.

I found out to my sorrow that this isn't the way alcohol works at all. You think you can turn it off and on any time you want to, but the time comes when it gets pretty tough to turn it off. The Lord knows, I had to learn this the hard way!

Well, this went on for awhile and finally, one night, my mother noticed that I had been drinking. So she went to my dad and said, "Fred, we're going to have to come up with something to keep that boy occupied and help keep him from gettin' into trouble. We don't want our son gettin' into the liquor. That would be disastrous."

My dad concurred in all this and said to me, "Edgar, what is it that you would like to do—something you would find some enjoyment in that would keep you occupied and help you stay out of trouble?"

I said, "Dad, do you know what I think I'd like to do? I think I'd like to get me a pony. If I could have a pony and a cart and could travel around the country and visit people... I'm gettin' a little tired of goin' to these shows and doin' stuff like that. This way, I could have something to do to keep myself occupied."

"All right," he said, "if you think that's what you need, we'll go up to Belmond and get you a pony." I had a relative up there who ran a pony farm.

So we went up to Belmond and my dad bought me a pony, along with a harness and cart, and we brought it all back to Rowan. I was very proud of the purchase we had just made.

As I told you, earlier, my dad owned the grain elevator in town and I kept my pony in a little barn right next to it, which he owned, also.

Well, I began to ride around the country, visiting with people I knew, and pretty soon my excursions began gettin' a little longer and longer. I was startin' to get home a little later at night than I should have.

After two or three of these occurrences, Dad called me aside and informed me in no uncertain terms that if I was goin' to have that pony out on the road, I was to have her back before dark, unharnessed and into the barn. I agreed to that. It sounded all right, and things went along pretty good for awhile. But pretty soon, it began to get a little later and later, again.

One night, it was really late when I got back home. I had been out in the country visitin' a friend by the name of Edward Drury. It was well after dark by the time I got to the barn and there stood my dad right by the door; and I noticed that he had a switch in his hand.

I sure didn't like the looks of all this; I knew there was trouble brewing, for sure.

"You get the harness off that pony," my dad instructed me, firmly, "and you get her into the barn and then we'll go home."

O.K., no problem. So I got her unharnessed and tethered properly in her stall in the barn. When I came out the door, Dad said, "Now we'll head for home." We were soon on our way.

As I mentioned earlier, the main street of Rowan was only about two blocks long, at least that portion of it that was business district. I was in favor of bypassing this direct route home. There were always people sittin' on those benches, and Uncle Frank would be one of them for sure.

"No," my dad said, "we won't go around nuthin'. We'll go straight down the middle of that street."

Well, man, imagine what was going to happen to my prestige, goin' down that street and passin' in front of those guys on the benches and my dad walkin' right behind me with that switch goin' swish, swish, swish, soundly switching my rear end every few steps. Boy, that was really embarrassing!

I walked right past the men on the benches summoning all the pride and indifference I could muster together. Just imagine, if you will, how I felt walkin' by Uncle Frank in particular, who was there, all right enough, wearin' a big grin on his face. I just knew he was thinkin', "Now I'll get even with this little scalawag for droppin' that snowball on my head."

There wasn't a darned thing I could do about this compromising situation, so I headed straight down the middle of that street, tryin' to hold my head up as best I could while Dad and I finished our trek on home and him layin' the switch to my butt all the while.

After I got home, I just couldn't bring myself to face these people for awhile. I was gonna' have to do something else. So I thought what I should do was to go down to Dows for a spell. My dad had a theater down there and a house that some people lived in where I could stay. So, I decided I was going to make myself scarce for awhile—such an embarrassing ordeal as I had just gone through.

I went down to Dows and stayed there for awhile. There was a girl down there who was about as tough as they could come, and she had some friends who weren't a helluva' lot better or less tough. I remember their names like it was only yesterday, but I guess it's best not to mention them here.

One day, three of us boys went out to the woods. I don't recall if we were huntin' squirrel or picking hickory nuts or just what, but anyway, we were out on the Iowa River north of Dows. As we came down the river, to our amazement when we looked up ahead, three girls were skinny dippin'; naked as blue jays.

Well, I'll tell you, here was the chance for some fun! Now we're going to steal their clothes and hide them, then hide behind a bush and wait to see what happens. We had overlooked the fact that this "tough" gal I mentioned a bit earlier might be one of the girls we were spyin' on. We had forgot that possibility. We had found something that was too exciting to be concerned about any consequences that might result from our prank.

We headed for the clothes layin' there on the river bank and we got up pretty close before that old girl spied us. And when she did, she came chargin' up outa' the water with her two companions right behind her.

I knew that if she ever caught us she would kill us for sure, so I took off. Didn't even stop to look at the scenery or nuthin'. When she got outa' the river, I was gone. That angry gal looked as big as a crippled rhinoceros, comin' up outa' that river; and boy, I was movin' out when she hit that bank. It didn't take too many smarts to figure out that the fire in her eyes boded no good for us intruders into their privacy.

I headed back to Dows, let me tell you, and when I got there, I decided it was time to go back to Rowan again. I had to figure that last escapade as a fluke. It didn't work out very well.

CHERRY BLOSSOM

Along about this time, something else took place in my life that was really exciting. My brother-in-law, who lived out north of Rowan, bought a race horse.

He lived out about three miles and I loved to stay with him because when he'd thresh or shell corn or something like that, I'd ride with him in his truck. He smoked cigarettes and when he'd get one smoked down part way, he'd give me the butt to finish off.

I'd sit there beside him in that truck and boy, I'll tell you, I was really sumthin'! I was doin' it just like the big boys, now—and lovin' every minute of it, y'know. And this is the way my smokin' habit got started.

As I said, my brother-in-law, Edgar Mantle, bought this race horse—a mare that answered to the name Cherry Blossom. Edgar was married to my sister, Marjorie, and I used to stay out there quite a bit. Well, I figured this was going to be something else—me gettin' a chance to ride on that race horse. "Bein' an experienced pony-man," I reasoned, "ridin' this bigger, faster animal should be a piece of cake! No problem at all."

Well, my brother-in-law kinda' thought I might get hurt on it, so he kept me off of Cherry Blossom for a long time. But I persisted in my hinting and coaxing and finally one day, he agreed to let me take her for a ride.

"All right, Edgar," my brother-in-law said to me, "I'm going to let you ride her. You can go up to the north pasture and get the cattle."

The pasture was up the road about a mile north of the house. I was instructed to go and get them, bring them down and put them in a pasture closer to home. He overlooked telling something about that race horse that he should have. If you squeezed her with your legs, she'd take off like the wind. That's the way race horses were trained back in those days, I guess.

Well, everything went O.K. gettin' up to the north pasture. Cherry Blossom wasn't exactly a thoroughbred but she was fast enough, believe me. In no time at all, we had those cattle rounded up, out through the gate and out onto the road headed for home.

We were about halfway home and everything was goin' smooth, when I inadvertently squeezed my legs against Cherry Blossom's ribs and when I did, all hell broke loose!

That filly took off like we was leavin' the starting gate at the Kentucky Derby. The next thing I knew, we were flyin' down that road like you can't believe. In order to keep from falling off, I had to squeeze her all the harder, y'know. I didn't know what else to do.

We were really makin' knots when we sailed into the driveway and when we made the turn, Cherry Blossom headed straight for the barn. The barn door was open and she charged full speed into the barn with me on her!

Well, this could have been a serious situation to get caught in, I'll tell you. I could have gotten hurt real bad. But I ducked down, goin' through that barn door, to keep my head from gettin' hit. Miraculously, we made it through O.K. with nobody the worse for it. As long as I didn't get hurt and no harm had come of the incident, I figured it best not to tell anyone about the happening; I would just keep it to myself, which I did.

Not too long after this, a horse race got promoted between my brother-in-law and a neighbor of his—fellow by the name of Jack Page. He had race horses, too. It was decided that I would be Cherry Blossom's jockey in the upcoming event.

A section of Highway Number 10 was marked off for the distance we were going to be racing. When we got over there on the morning of the race, a crowd of spectators was already beginning to arrive on the scene. An air of excitement could be felt settling all around the place as the time for the race to start drew near.

Well, I'm up there on Cherry Blossom, proud as punch. I'm right up there amongst the big shots again! When the starting pistol was fired, we took off, right down that highway, hellbent for leather!

Down the road apiece ahead of us, my folks had a rather large garden plot that they had planted earlier. When Cherry Blossom and I came abreast of the driveway, she turned into it without warning, jumping the closed gate at full speed. Well, Edgar Brooks, the would-be-jockey, went straight on ahead!

I lit in a pile of debris of some sort that had been raked up in the immediate area, wound up with one arm broken and was badly skinned up. I decided, then and there, that I'd had enough of the horse racing bit. No more riding race horses for me. I could see where that could be a pretty tough way to win fame and fortune, y'know!

POPCORN MACHINE

With my injured arm sort of keepin' me out of the running for awhile, boredom commenced setting in on me again. I was at a loss to find meaningful ways to fill my time, it seemed. The next thing I knew, I had gone back to nippin' just a little bit. I was tired of goin' to those shows all the time and I needed something to fill the vacuum.

I think my mother might have noticed I was imbibing a bit in the liquid refreshments and she commenced getting on Dad to do something. Dad called me aside along about then and said, "Edgar, I believe I know of something you might like to do. I know a man down at Dows who has a popcorn machine. Why don't we go down there and get it and set it up in front of the theater and you can sell popcorn. Maybe, you'd enjoy doing that."

Oh boy! That sounded pretty good! So we went down to Dows and got the popcorn machine and set it out in front of the theater, there on Main Street.

Now, this popcorn machine had glass all around it. It stood on wheels and you stood outside of it to operate the popper, fill the sacks of popcorn for the customers, etc. In no time, things were goin' pretty darned good. I was a business man, right up there with the other business people in Rowan.

Everything had its place inside the glass enclosure of the popcorn machine—the salt containers stacked on one side, the butter container on the opposite side, all within handy reach. When a customer ordered a bag of popcorn, I would dash some salt into it, pour on some hot butter and exchange it for the five cents it took to buy it back in those days. Lots of times, they would say, "Put on a little more butter," so I would give 'em some more butter; no problem. I was happy to oblige.

I was usin' so much butter that my popcorn machine began to get all smeared up with butter, inside. One evening the alcohol burner that popped the corn caught that accumulation of butter on fire. Oh boy! Now we was havin' some real excitement goin'!

Now, Edgar Mantle, my brother-in-law who had the race horse, was there when all this happened. He went one way and I went the other and let 'er burn. No way was I gonna' take a chance gettin' burned trying to put out that fire, so we just let 'er burn out. Later, my brother-in-law and I came back, pulled what was left of the machine around behind the building and let 'er set there. That was the end of my first business experience. I didn't want no more of that! I decided I would leave the popcorn machine enterprise for somebody else.

COON HUNTING

My older brother, George, got acquainted with some folks out in the country who had some coon dogs. They hunted coons a lot out in the timber along the Iowa River.

One time, when they were going to go coon huntin' at night, they invited George to go along. I don't remember exactly how I got myself into that thing but, anyway, I made it some way.

A small group of us went out into the woods with them bayin' dogs in tow. They built a big fire and we were all sittin' around this fire waitin' for those hounds to dig up sumthin'.

Suddenly, I heard something a comin' down through the woods for real. Boy, this coon dog had hit a trail right behind me! He let out a howl that scared me half to death! I went straight up in the air, not knowing for sure just exactly what was happening!

"He's trackin' a coon," someone ventured. "Let's try to follow him."

Well, that dog was hot on the trail of

sumthin', all right, and it turned out to be a skunk! Man, you shoulda' smelled that dog! He stunk to high heaven and I had to ride home alongside that bugger in the back seat!

Before we started for home, one of the other dogs hit a coon track and we all took out in hot pursuit after him. We followed him maybe a mile or two through those dark woods and pretty soon the dog ran the coon up a tree. Then, one of the guys shot the frightened animal down outa' that tree. He came tumblin' down out of the tree and hit the ground with a thud. The men put him in a sack and we took him home with us. When we got there, the Card brothers skinned him out. I had never seen that done before.

A coon supper was put on the agenda for the following Saturday night. Mrs. Card, the young men's mother, was going to cook up the raccoon and we'd all have a big feed.

George and I were invited to come out for the event. So, we went out to Card's place and fiddled around a bit for awhile in the evening until Mrs. Card made the announcement that it was time to eat. My brother and I were washing' our faces when I felt George pokin' me in the ribs.

I remember thinking, "What in the world does he want?" My eyes are full of soap and I can't see nuthin'; and I'm groping around, blindly in search of something to wipe my face with. What I turned up with was a nice lace curtain rather than a towel!

Here I am, wipin' my face on one of Mrs. Card's good curtains, and that got my brother riled up a little. He laid it on me good. I never did find out why he poked me in the ribs in the first place. I just chalked it up to one more of little Edgar's classical screw-ups.

George and I had occasion to go out to the

Card farm for another coon hunt, sometime after that. The dogs hit the trail of a big coon and were in hot pursuit of the fleeing animal when he ran headlong down into a pond of water with the hounds right after him. That was the wrong thing for those eager dogs to do. Coons are very vicious animals when cornered. They'll grab a dog by the nose and pull him right underneath the water until he's dead. When the melee that resulted in that pond was over, the coon had drowned all three of the dogs that had been chasing it!

I dunno'—seems like I was always gettin' into something.

HOLLYWOOD BOUND?

From time to time, I used to appear in stage shows, such as "Uncle Tom's Cabin," at Dad's theater. As my part in the performance, I would dance. I used to dance the Charleston pretty well.

One day I decided that I would go over to Alden, where my dad had a big ballroom, and dance the Charleston. Alden was about 20 miles away, so I stayed with some people there.

Well, this idea of mine got to goin' pretty well. I'd get into the old ballroom and do the Charleston for the folks quite frequently. People would form a ring around me and throw nickels and dimes, even quarters sometimes, on the dance floor, and things were going pretty good.

This thing was payin' off pretty well, except my dad wasn't cotton'n up to this new enterprise of mine too heartily. He didn't approve of the performance I was puttin' on for his customers. But on the other hand, he felt that if it would help serve as a deterrent against my

maybe gettin' back to nippin' booze again,
maybe he shouldn't interfere. So, I kept doin'
my Charleston act and gettin' paid for it for
some time.

One day, a man from Hollywood walked into
Dad's dance hall and watched the performance
for awhile. Then, he asked my dad to come into
the office to discuss my act. I think Dad had
gotten acquainted with this fellow sometime
prior to all this, I'm not sure just how. Dad's
acquaintanceships were pretty broad in those
days, what with all of the diverse enterprises he
was involved in so much of the time.

Dad was really surprised to learn what this
fellow had in mind. I guess Dad thought it was
going to be some sort of business deal.

"Fred," the visitor addressed my father when
they had closed the office door behind them, "I
would like to take that kid of yours to Hollywood
and give him a screen test. He's doin' pretty well
out there."

"Well, I dunno'," my dad hesitated. "I'll go
have a little chat with Edgar."

So, he came out and said to me, "Son, we've
got a man out here from Hollywood and he
would like for you to go out there with him and
take a screen test. Would you like to go down
there?"

"Well, I should say not! Why would I go to
Hollywood when I got things goin' as good as
they are, right here at home? No way!"

Perhaps I goofed an opportunity there that
was fantastic; and it kinda' seems, sometimes,
that I've been goofin' them ever since....

O'LEARY LAKE SCHOOL, 1928

5

Coming to Buck Lake

Things went along pretty nicely for me until 1928 when the Big Depression hit the country. When that depression hit, my dad lost almost everything he owned.

Dad had already been through one nervous breakdown, sometime earlier. He had been taken to Battle Creek, Michigan, in a straight jacket for a cure. We had hoped that this sort of thing would never happen again, but now, once again, we had cause for concern that it might happen all over again. He lost the farms, our home, the grain elevators, his theaters and one of the two skating rinks. He lost everything but one big ballroom and believe me, this let-down hit my dad mighty hard. Fortunately, Dad hung in there emotionally this time.

One of his most costly losses was the grain elevators. It was customary in that business to grant credit to the neighborhood farmers to enable them to buy seed for the spring planting and feed for their livestock during the summer months. When fall came, they would sell their livestock and pay their feed bills.

When that depression hit, they couldn't sell their stock and pay what they owed the elevator. Hog and cattle prices had dropped to practically nothing.

"Fred," one farmer said to my dad, "I can't make it; but if you want some of these hogs, help yourself." So my dad got a carload of this fellow's hogs and shipped them to Chicago. They paid him one cent per pound for them. It wasn't even enough to pay the freight bill to the railroad.

Those who got caught up in its devastating ramifications will never forget the Depression of the Thirties. The Great Depression probably changed the course of more people's lives than any other single event in the history of our country, with the possible exception of World War II.

HARD TIMES

The dilemma that the Fred Brooks family now found itself facing with the sudden collapse of Dad's financial empire held little in the way of available options. There just wasn't a whole lot that Dad could do to ameliorate the hardships our family faced in the foreseeable future.

Somehow, we managed to salvage the large ballroom in Alden when Dad's creditors foreclosed on all of his other holdings. Dad traded his ballroom to the Johnson Land Company for 960 acres of unimproved land up here in northern Minnesota, with the understanding that we could exchange 360 acres of it for a like number of acres that they owned in the area, at our discretion.

In January or February of 1928, we came up to take a good look at the situation. We lived in a tent for about one month. Imagine living in a tent during weather temperatures of anywhere from 20 degrees to 40 degrees below zero and burning wood to keep warm! One person would stay up around the clock while the rest of the family slept near the stove. During that month, Dad did make the exchange for 360 acres of land in a location of his choosing and we returned to Iowa.

When we got back to Rowan, we loaded up a boxcar with all of our personal possessions, which included some machinery, my pony and a roller skating rink that could be disassembled and moved. The skating rink was one of two we had owned and operated in Iowa. Dad had salvaged it along with the ballroom that had now been traded for land in Minnesota.

We had decided to live in Nashwauk for the remainder of the winter and Dad had made arrangements with the proper authorities there to operate the skating rink when we arrived. We brought two big tents with us. One of the tents housed the rink and we lived in the other one. When we finally got settled into our new surroundings, Dad had just $15 left in his pocket. Needless to say, things were pretty tight, financially, for awhile.

After we got moved, one of the first things I discovered was that alcohol did the same thing for me here in Minnesota that it did in Iowa, and I was pleased with that.

Now don't get me wrong, folks; I was no soak, no real heavy drinker or anything like that. I was too young to be into it that far. I was around 14 years of age at that time but admittedly, I liked a nip or two occasionally. It seemed to do something for me a little better than anything else I could find in the way of nourishing my ego and general feeling of well-being.

We got the roller skating rink put up there in Nashwauk and we lived in the second tent. In due time, we brought a third tent to our land north of Buck Lake to use while we were building our log house for a permanent residence. We had decided to build the house out of logs because it was the only way we could afford to do it. The trees needed to make logs were readily available right there on our own property.

As soon as the weather permitted, we started cutting trees and dragging the logs out of the woods. We piled them up until they could be properly trimmed and notched before assembling them into the walls of the house. With the entire family involved in the undertaking, we accomplished our objective in record time and eventually got relocated from the tent in Nashwauk into our new home, which served our purpose very well.

First deer

Shortly after we got our house built, I had my first deer hunting experience. My folks had some friends come up from Iowa and we took them out hunting. A man who lived over west of us went along with us. He was on the deer stand and I was one of those making the drive.

All of a sudden, a buck ran by me and, man, he was really a sailin'! I was shootin' a shotgun with buckshot loaded in it. Ka-bang! I cut loose on him but missed, or so I thought at the time.

The buck went on by in the direction of our neighbor who had stationed himself up on a side hill some distance from where I was. I heard a loud BOOM! BOOM! BOOM! as he shot three times, finally knocking the fleeing animal down. I immediately ran up to where he was standing over the fallen deer and told him how I had shot at the buck but had apparently missed it.

We eviscerated the dead animal and took it to my folks' place to skin it out. It was at that time that we discovered I had been laboring under the misconception that I had missed the deer and that my neighbor had finally killed it. It turned out that there were only two buckshot holes in him and they had come from my gun, since my neighbor was using a rifle. It was my shooting that had really done the trick. A wounded deer can sometimes run quite a distance after it has been mortally wounded, which was the case in this instance.

The buck's having finally fallen dead right after my neighbor had cut loose on it was mere coincidence. Be that as it may, this sort of spoiled my first experience at hunting deer; sort of took the excitement out of it for me.

ELECTRIC FENCE

In due time, my dad got a small herd of cattle started and along about that same time, my mom commenced gettin' a flock of layin' hens established. We were gradually gettin' our affairs set up to enable us to live off the land, in a manner of speaking.

A neighbor, who lived about two miles north of our place, had a rather large herd of cattle, including a bull that was about the meanest thing you ever saw. Sometimes around midnight, we'd hear that bull comin' down the road bellerin' up a storm, "B-r-r-r, b-r-r-r, m-o-oa!" Everybody would get up out of bed and be ready for him when he got there.

We had a big police dog at this time who could handle this bull pretty good. So, when this bull would get to our place, we'd turn the dog loose on him and when we did, all hell would break loose outside. Eventually, the uninvited intruder would go back home only to come back again the next night.

Dad soon discovered he was going to have to put up an electric fence. Now, we had a boy staying at our place at this time, makin' his home with us. The electric fence Dad had put up to keep our cattle in and the neighbor's cattle out kind of intrigued us. So, we decided to test out this electric fence on Ma's chickens.

We proceeded to put a few insulators out on the ground near the chicken house. Then, we put a pan of wet mash out on those insulators and connected all this to the electric fence with a strand of wire. What we had in mind was to shock Ma's ol' rooster, who had a tendency to be a little on the cocky side as he strutted his stuff among all those hens.

This rooster had different ideas, despite all of our well-laid plans. He would come up to that bowl of wet mash and commence crowing at the top of his voice, "Coo-ra! Coo-ra!" That was his way of coaxing all the hens in there close. This old boy was a real hunk, no doubt about it!

Well, one of the old hens walked over and poked her nose into that pan of wet mash. When that jolt of electricity hit her, she leaped about a foot into the air and her loud "A-a-wk, a-a-k!" cackling sent the rest of the flock scurrying for parts elsewhere. Then she squatted down and proceeded to lay an egg! It was the darndest sight you ever saw. You can be sure Ma never found out the truth about that "lone chicken egg we found out there in the grass someplace."

IGNUS

One resource we did not lack when we came here was timber. Boy, we had lots of that! Dad had acquired a sawmill early on and moved it out onto our land. A man named Ignus Gressick operated the mill. I think my dad and Ignus had formed some sort of partnership in the sawmill business; I'm not sure. Ignus was a nice fellow, but he talked real slow; just b-a-r-e-l-y kept the flow of words comin' when he was conversing.

Ignus had occasion to drive down to Minneapolis to get some needed supplies one day. When he got back, my dad asked him how the trip had gone.

"Oh, Fred," Ignus slowly replied, "it ... was ... pretty ... bad. That ... road ... was ... purty ... darned ... icy. I ... got ... down ... the ... other ... side ... of ... Cloquet, came ... down ... a ... hill ... and ... around ... a ... corner ... and ... my car started spinnin' round ... and ... around ... and when it finally ... came ... to ... a ... stop, I had to go to a farmer's ... house ... to find out ... which ... way ... it was to ... Minneapolis." That was Ignus for you.

SCHOOL

Well, we started cutting timber and between the roller skating rink and the lumber operation, things began to look up again. A few dollars were beginning to come in and we could finally buy things we needed but couldn't afford since things had gone bad back in Iowa.

So now, my folks had to start thinkin' about gettin' me back in school. I soon started to attend the O'Leary Lake School. It was about two miles north of our place and I would walk to and from school, sometimes in weather that reached 40 degrees below zero. The school teacher boarded with my folks during the school term and she would walk with me. The old school was nothing but a tar paper shack.

By the time I started the following school year, a new school building had been built at Buck Lake. It was a nice little one-room building and now we only had to walk a mile and a quarter to get to school.

After I had attended classes there for some time, I took my savings from working in the sawmill for my dad and Ignus and bought me another pony. We built a little barn down near the schoolhouse to put it in during school hours, so now I could ride to school instead of having to walk, which was great. I liked school a lot better, then.

This new school was located about 300 feet from a bootlegger's place. Now, with this added attraction, I was commencin' to really feel comfortable around school—likin' it better all the time. When the opportunity presented itself, I would sneak over to that bootlegger's place for a couple of snifters; and when I'd come back to school, some pretty interesting and exciting things would sometimes take place, I can assure you.

The schoolroom was heated with a wood burning stove and we boys would carry in wood the night before for the following morning. The next morning when we'd come to school, we'd light the fire in the stove. While one of us was gettin' the fire going, the other one would crawl up onto the roof of the building and put a board over the chimney—sometimes even sit on it. Of course, when we got the fire lit, the darned stove would start to smoke. The teacher couldn't quite figure out what was causin' all this and of course, us boys were puzzled about all this, too!

That old pot-bellied stove would be belchin' smoke in every direction and nuthin' we did to stop it seemed to help. When this happened, the teacher would decide that we couldn't have school that day, what with all that smoke was fillin' the room, so school would be canceled for the day. Of course, us boys would feel awfully bad about havin' the whole day ahead of us to do with as we pleased! We'd go home and come back the next day and would you believe, some new problem would show up!

Back in those days, at least in the school I was going to, we prepared our own ink for putting into those little glass inkwells built into the top of each desk. We mixed it in a half-gallon pail that sat behind the stove to make sure it didn't freeze in cold weather, I suppose. When it came time to refill the little individual glass inkwells, the ink supply would be poured into several glass bottles and a cork placed in the neck of each bottle.

Some of us guys had gotten ahold of some carbide; and just before it came time to fill these bottles, we would pour a little carbide into the bottles, on the sly. When we poured the ink from the pail into these bottles and put the cork in, the cork would start risin' right up out of the neck of that bottle. Nobody but us boys who were putting the carbide in the bottles before filling them with ink knew what was the matter.

So, someone would stuff the cork back again; and pretty soon it would commence rising up out of the bottle neck. Each time this occurred, the cork would be replaced a bit more firmly than the time before. And after a bit, "Kapooie!" That bottle would explode and spew ink all over the place, and us guys would get a big kick out of that!

Sometimes when that pail of ink was sittin' behind the stove, it would get warm and commence to foam. The teacher would scratch her head tryin' to figure out what this was all about, too. I don't know if she ever figured out that us boys had put a little carbide in the pail when she wasn't looking.

It wasn't just the boys who liked to play tricks on the teacher, however. Sometimes, when we were outside at recess or noon hour, all of us kids would play a trick on her. When she rang the bell summoning us to come back inside, no one would show up. Then, after a bit, she would go outside and commence looking around the schoolhouse for us.

I don't know why she never discovered that the schoolhouse was sittin' about two feet up off the ground on some kind of concrete supports. All of us kids would be on the far side of the building when she came out lookin' for us. We could peek through the space beneath the building and see her feet a'goin'. Then, we would scurry around the opposite side of the school-house from where she was at the moment and just keep goin' round and around ahead of her.

As a last resort, she would go down to the lake to see if we were down there and when she'd get back, there we'd be in the classroom all properly seated at our desks.

"Where in the world have you kids been?" she would inquire of us.

"Why, we've been right here, ma'am," we would answer. Then, she would take her place behind her desk with a puzzled look on her face and resume her duties as though nothing had happened.

Once in awhile, the gang would go down to that cussed lake and go swimming. On such occasions, we always swam in our birthday suits. Then, she'd come stormin' down there to route us out of the water. When we saw her comin' we would all duck beneath the water so she couldn't see us, and after taking a quick look and seeing no one, she would stomp back to the schoolhouse muttering veiled threats beneath her breath. Then, we would all get dressed and traipse back to school.

There was always something out of the ordinary going on around that place, it seemed. I sometimes think that goin' to that particular school had something to do with me bein' so smart (chuckle)! I acquired quite an education for myself attending that academic institution.

One of the best things that ever happened in my life happened there in that school. I met a little girl when I was in the fifth grade and she went all the way through school with me. In fact, she has gone all through life with me and this year (1992), on March 21, we had our fifty-seventh wedding anniversary. It's a mystery to me why she is still on the scene, after some of the things that have happened during our life together, but the good part of all this is that she's still here. She always said I was too ornery to live with, but I was too lovely to throw out, so she just kept me around here.

Eventually, we graduated from that old school. There was some talk of burning the place down to get rid of me, but they didn't have to resort to such a radical plan as that. I finally made it O.K., and that was the end of my formal schooling. The eighth grade was as far as I ever got.

Allie went on and got more schooling in Grand Rapids, but I felt like it was time for me to go home and help my dad now. Things were still a bit tough at times and he was workin' hard to clear off more land of trees, gettin' a barn built and building up a larger herd of cattle. I figured he needed all the help he could get.

COWBOYS AND BIG TRUCKS

It was along about this time, 1931 or 1932, I think, that a severe drought hit the western states. With no hay to feed their cattle, the ranchers were facing the dilemma of their cattle dying off from starvation. In desperation, a delegation of ranchers contacted farmers here in Minnesota. They had a representative come and talk to the people here to find out if an arrangement could be worked out for them to transport their cattle out here to get them through the summer.

A deal was struck whereby they would pay three dollars a head to farmers who would pasture their cattle through the bad time. So, my dad ordered 3,000 of these western steers and several of our neighbors took on 2,000 or 3,000 head, also.

While we were waiting for the cattle to come, my dad and I went to Grand Rapids, where I traded off my pony for a larger saddle horse. I figured if I was going to be a cowboy for real, I had to have a real cow pony to ride.

It wasn't too long until all those cattle arrived in Nashwauk by train. So a bunch of us rode our saddle horses into town, unloaded the cattle from the rail cars and herded them out to our place where they were placed in a large corral for the night.

The Browns, who lived north of us, had ordered several thousand, too, so they helped us make the drive that day. We finally got them home O.K., but I want to tell you, that was one herd of wild, ugly-dispositioned cattle—fresh off the range and not used to folks being around much.

We had a fellow helping us by the name of Einer Heininen. There was one old cow with only one horn and she took out after him with blood in her eye. He jumped beneath a truck, which probably saved his life.

The following morning, we turned those western cattle loose from the enclosure they had been confined to during the night and got them situated into the pastures where they were to be kept that summer. I'll tell you, that summer was one of the liveliest ones I can recall at that stage of my life.

Those cattle got into farmers' haystacks all over the neighborhood. They smashed down fences and wandered away from their home pastures, and then would have to be rounded up and herded back home and the fences repaired. Occasionally, some of them would get mired down in floating bogs—sometimes referred to as sinkholes—and go completely under.

Not all of the dead cattle we would find out in the woods were a result of their drowning in those bogs. We would find some lyin' out there that had been shot. Whenever we found where somebody had helped themselves to a steer to have beef to eat, we would cut the brand off and save it as evidence. Doing this was a bit messy, but it served to verify the numbers that were involved in the contract with those western ranchers.

That eventful summer finally passed. When we got all those cattle rounded up to herd them back to Nashwauk and get them loaded on the trains, a considerable shortage had occurred for various reasons. But all-in-all, the whole venture proved satisfactory for everyone involved. We had picked up some extra cash in the deal and the ranchers had their cattle back with more meat on their ribs than when they had sent them to Minnesota. And by this time, some fall rains had provided the needed moisture to restore the range grass.

With the job of ridin' herd on all those cattle over now, I went to work in my dad's sawmill full-time.

Somewhere along about this time, my dad bought a truck. A county job had opened up and my dad was hired as the foreman, overseeing the graveling of the county roads. My brother, George, drove Dad's truck for quite awhile—a year or so—when we were working for the county. Eventually, we began using it at the sawmill, hauling lath and other things. The locomotives used in the iron mines provided a good market for locomotive kindling and we hauled wood suitable for that purpose all up and down the Iron Range. Sometime later, George got a job with the State Highway Commission and when he did, I took over driving the truck.

I guess I was 15, maybe 16 years of age at the time. I was really too young to be driving the truck out on the highway, but I got by okay and I followed this line of work for the next several years.

ALLIE

Allie and I had been going together steady ever since grade school days. We were married when I was about 19. Dad gave us 160 acres of land that was part of his larger parcel of land as a wedding present. The whole family pitched in and helped build a house on it. So now, Allie and I found ourselves engaged in the business of farming.

Some of the folks around the country, knowin' me as they did, said, "That marriage will never work. It'll be a fluke for sure." Well, folks, it has worked for more than 57 years, now, and I'm in hopes that it might continue. Allie has never talked divorce, but she has considered murder several times!

We were married by a Lutheran minister my dad knew back in Iowa. Before moving to Grand Rapids, this minister had lived on a road several miles out north of Rowan, Iowa, where I was born. This road was called Snarl Street, not because it was a crooked road or street, but because of the caliber of folks who had settled on it in years gone by—a pretty rough lot, according to legend. Feuding between neighbors was goin' on much of the time, sort of like the Hatfields and the McCoys back in Kentucky in the old days, I guess. Snarl Street was really a country road that followed the north bank of the Iowa River for several miles, extending eastward from Highway 69.

My folks, my Uncle Ed and his family, another guy by the name of Flip Harrigan and his family, and maybe another family or two all lived out there on Snarl Street together at one time. My folks moved to town eventually, before I was born. To this day, everyone around Rowan can tell you about Snarl Street; and every one of them will have a different version about that legendary thoroughfare, I'll venture.

Well, we threw a wing-ding of a party after our wedding. Then, a little later, we were shivareed at my folks' house. Boy, what a jamboree that turned out to be!

My brother-in-law, Chet Moellering, and my sister, had moved up to Buck Lake, too, by this time. Chet wasn't the brother-in-law I mentioned earlier, who furnished me with cigarettes at threshing time. Chester didn't drink or do any of that sort of thing.

Apparently, my teetotalling brother-in-law felt this to be a special occasion, for he permitted himself to indulge by taking on a few hookers of hard liquor that night. Pretty soon we began to see a side of Chester that no one had ever seen previously. We had him dancing with snowshoes on in the middle of the living room and really joining in on the fun that all the rest of us were having. I'm not sure how he felt the next day, but he was sure livin' it up that night.

Some folks by the name of Kreps ran the store down at Buck Lake. A few days after our wedding, they decided to put on a second party for Allie and me. This one turned out to be even wilder than the first one. It was a beautiful evening when we first got there, but by the time we got ready to leave for home in the middle of the night, it was snowing. It had accumulated to a depth of 12 inches or more during the party, making the roads slippery and treacherous to drive upon, I vividly recall. So the date of March 21, 1935 is a special milestone in both Allie's life and mine, and lots of water has flowed over the dam during the 57 years that have ensued.

Allie's
Story

AILI AND ALLIE PERATALO

6

Take care of yourself

(As told by Allie Peratalo Brooks)

My brother, Arthur, and I were born in Hibbing, Minnesota on March 14, 1915 to our parents, Charlie and Anna Peratalo. My twin brother died at a very young age. I'm not sure just how old he was when this happened, as my folks didn't talk much about it. I only weighed four pounds at birth, so perhaps I was fortunate to survive. There were no high-tech medical facilities to handle this sort of thing back in those days.

My parents moved from Hibbing to a little farm, only two and one-half miles from Buck Lake where Edgar and I are living as I write this. My folks were from Finland where my oldest brother, Arvi, was born. Auno, my next oldest brother, and Aili, my older sister, were born in this country. Then, next in the line of succession came my twin brother and me.

I am full blood Finn. I learned to talk Finn as a child, which always made it easy for me to communicate with those people in our peer group who couldn't speak English. This always made me fell good and probably explains why I got along well with the people around me all of my life.

I'm not as fluent in Finn as I used to be because I don't have occasion to use the language as much as I did when I was younger. Most of the local folks who conversed in that language have passed away.

My father was a very strict man. I don't recall his ever really spanking us kids. All he had to do was look at us and tell us what we had to do, and we did it, no questions asked.

We grew up with the saying, "First you work, then you play." We didn't have electricity; we didn't have a telephone, no oil heaters; so there were many chores around the place that were the responsibility of us kids. We carried wood for the stoves and we carried water in pails from an outside pump for drinking, doing the dishes and washing clothes. The lamps had to be filled with kerosene every few days and, of course, there was always the ultra-modern facility commonly called the "slop jar" that had to be carried out a reasonable distance from the house and dumped. This little porcelain receptacle, with lid to match, was kept under the bed and saved us from having to make the trip to the outdoor privy when nature called during the night hours. When we caught up on the tasks around the house, there were always chores to perform out around the barnyard.

As a very young child, I started assuming what today would be considered adult responsibilities. I was doing the dishes and house cleaning; and then a little later, I started doing the family washing on a scrub board. This took all day and wasn't all that good for the shoulders and back.

We had to boil the white clothes to make sure they didn't have any "tattletale gray" color, then take them outdoors and hang them on the clothesline in the back yard. In the wintertime, my fingers were nearly frozen by the time this task was completed.

In addition to all this, we had cattle, horses, chickens and sheep that needed caring for at least twice daily. In the morning, we milked the cows and put hay in the mangers for them to eat. After that was done, the chickens had to be fed.

In the afternoon, the cattle had to be watered. There was a swamp pond behind the barn that would freeze over in the wintertime, making it necessary for us to chop a big hole in the ice so the livestock could drink water. While they were out drinking water, we would put hay in their mangers. Each cow had her own stall and woe be to any cow that tried to slip into another cow's place on the sly!

After the cows and calves were all back in the barn, we would let the horses out. While they were out drinking from the hole in the ice, we cleaned their stalls and put hay in their mangers. Then, later in the afternoon, it would be milking time. On more than one occasion, I lost a toenail because a cow had stepped on my foot. My mother would tell me, "You learn, this way, to watch out; to take care of yourself."

My sister and I had to do the chores around our place because my dad was loggin' out in the woods from early 'til late nearly every day. He also cut firewood and sold it. My mother and brothers worked out there with Dad, so the farm chores got shuttled off onto my sister and me.

When I was six years old, I started attending classes at the Daybrook School. We lived by the Daybrook River. In the fall when school opened, I would walk to the river, row our boat across it and then walk the rest of the distance, which was about a mile and a half in all. Then, when school was out that afternoon, I'd walk back to the river again, take the boat across and finish the trip back home on foot.

My mom and dad knew about what time I would be coming home, so they would watch for me. They didn't let me know they were doing this or that they were concerned about me, because they wanted us kids to learn to watch out for ourselves. They would always say, "Watch out that you don't get hurt," and I was taught not to be afraid when I was walking to and from school.

When winter came and the river froze over, I would walk across it on the ice instead of depending on the rowboat. Later in the the winter, the deep snowdrifts would block my trail. When this happened, I had to walk the roads. The roads were plowed out by the county road maintenance crews. Taking this route required me to walk two and one-half miles each way, but I didn't mind because it was easier walking.

When I got a little older, I learned how to snare rabbits, which was lots of fun. In the mornings, I would nearly always see deer along the way. Once in awhile I would see a weasel, but I don't recall ever having seen a bear during my daily walks to school.

I'm left-handed, so I had some problems when I started to school. The teacher wouldn't let me write left-handed. She slapped my fingers with a ruler more than once until I learned to write right-handed.

Penmanship was taught in school those days as a separate subject. Most schoolteachers back then considered writing left-handed a handicap that had to be overcome, so I endeavored doubly hard to learn to write with my right hand instead of my left. I felt quite proud when I had accomplished this objective. I also learned to knit and crochet right-handed, but I do most everything else left-handed to this day.

While I was attending school, my parents relieved me of having to do the chores that I mentioned earlier, with the exception of doing dishes, because they wanted to be sure that I got my school homework done. In addition to my regular lessons, I brought books home from the library, which I read every night. I loved fairy tales.

My dad and mom were very good dancers. Dances were sometimes held in the schoolhouses in our area and my folks never missed one of them if it was at all possible for them to go. Usually, the whole family would go with them. They had a sleigh equipped with blankets, quilts and pillows placed above a layer of hay for insulation from the cold and we kids would cuddle up close together under those blankets as warm as toast. I can still hear in my mind the squeaky, singing sound the runners of the sleigh made as they passed over the packed snow.

The horse's harness was trimmed with bells and tassels and Dad would braid the horse's tail and tie it up neatly. All of us felt we were really in style with all those bells tinkling and the harness ornaments sparkling in the moonlight as we trotted briskly over the roads to the school dances.

My dad taught me to dance while I was still quite young. Waltzes, polkas and the schottische were the popular steps in those days.

When automobiles started to make the scene, my dad bought a car and a truck. The truck was used for logging. The car was used mostly to go shopping in town and for visiting with neighbors, which was a custom in those days, particularly on Sunday afternoons.

My folks usually worked at logging five days each week. On Saturday, Mom and Dad would go to town to do their shopping. Dad did some drinking on these occasions, so it usually took them all day before they got home.

My sister and I would do all the chores, then have supper ready when they returned. If there was a dance anywhere, Dad would see to it that we girls got there. Sometimes my older brother would ask my dad if he could use the car to go to the show in town. My dad usually gave him permission to use the car, providing he took my sister and me along so we could see the show, too. We would laugh about this because we knew he wanted to go alone, as he had a girl-friend.

I remember one time my brother asked to use the car and Dad let him have it to go see his girlfriend. What my brother didn't know was that Dad had checked the mileage on the odometer before he left. The next day my dad asked him where he had gone. My brother's answer didn't jibe with the mileage on the odometer and he got grounded for some time.

You didn't lie to my dad. We were taught that there was to be no lying, no stealing and no swearing. We were taught to have respect for our elders and no back talk. The folks could take us to visit in anyone's house and we would behave ourselves; never got into trouble. This all went back to discipline in one's upbringing and I thank my dad immensely for this.

Being poor, my mom had to learn to do many things for herself and I have been inclined to follow her pattern. I paid quite a bit of attention to my elders and learned from them as I was growing up. I would say (and I still say it today), "If you can do it, so can I." All my life I've believed that people can accomplish most anything they want to do if they set their minds to it in earnest.

We didn't have lots of toys, as today's children have. Today, children take so many things for granted. I had just one small doll. We had only one sled, which we kids had to share between us. We had ice skates that clamped onto our boots and were tightened with a little key-like wrench so they wouldn't come off while we were skating. Sometimes, these skates would pull the soles of our shoes away from the uppers. Then Dad would have to slip them upside down over a metal shoe last and nail the soles back on again. So much in the way of repair work was done right at home in those days.

We lived on a high hill and in the winter when there was snow on the ground, we would slide down the steep slopes in cardboard boxes or on a sheep hide. We learned to ski the hard way on those hills; our skis were made of barrel staves strapped to our feet. I took many a nasty spill streaking down the hill on those homemade skis, but eventually got pretty good at it and have always enjoyed skiing as a winter sport.

During the summer months, my sister and I would take the boat out to the middle of the river and put out the anchor. Then, we would jump in and go swimming. The bottom of the river was muddy, but we didn't care. There would be leeches swimming around us and occasionally we would get a blood sucker on a toe. I found one attached to my little toe one time and when I pulled it off, the blood squirted out in a fine stream. I held my finger against the spot where the blood was coming out and after awhile it stopped.

As I said earlier, we were brought up not to be afraid of anything. When we got hurt, we did for ourselves, if we could, right there at home. We didn't run to a doctor every time we got hurt. Couldn't afford to, even though doctors didn't charge nearly as much for their services in those days as they do now. If you really needed a doctor, you didn't go to his office or to a hospital. Instead, he would come to your house.

My brother and I played a game on our front porch called mumble peg. With one blade fully opened and the other blade opened only halfway, a knife was flipped into the air. The score was based on whether or not one or more of the open blades stuck into the wood floor. If it fell on its side, there was no score. You had to be careful how you flipped the knife because it was done with the blades being held between the thumb and index finger. I cut my finger many times playing mumble peg before I learned how to hold the knife just right when flipping it. Another one of our homespun activities was walking on stilts made by my brother.

I changed schools when I was in the fifth grade. We lived between two different schools and I had the choice of whichever one I wanted to attend. I had to walk two and one-half miles to get to school and as I got closer to school, other kids would join me. Then, we would walk

Buck Lake School, 1929

together the rest of the way, talking up a storm all the while.

It was during one of these treks to school that someone asked me if I knew Edgar Brooks. I said, "No, who is he?" They told me all about him and where he lived. I knew most of the other kids, so I soon figured out who he was by the process of elimination.

The kids all liked Edgar because he talked all the time. Being the quiet type, that didn't impress me much, but we all got along fine in school. I was assigned the desk right behind him, wouldn't you know!

There was lots of whispering taking place in this new school amongst the students and this was something I wasn't used to. My dad had

89

always told me that in school, teacher was boss...and not to forget it.

Lots of parents, especially fathers, had a sort of unwritten law that they laid down for their children of school age: "If you get a lickin' in school by the teacher for something you've done wrong, you can expect to get another one just like it when you get home." I don't recall my dad saying that in so many words, but he always told me that while I was in school, the teacher was boss and when I was home, he was the boss! So I didn't make a practice of taking home with me anything of adverse nature that happened in school that day.

One Saturday, my sister and I were skating with some kids from a logging camp that was close to our place. My mom came running across the field to the top of the hill within earshot of where we were skating. Cupping her mouth in her hands, she shouted down to us at the top of her voice, "Come quick! Dad is dead!"

We tore our skates off, frantically, and headed for home. There was a nurse in the logging camp and she came along with us. On our way home, Mom explained to us what had happened.

Dad had been plowing snow off the road across the field with a team of horses. My mom noticed the horses standing still in the same spot for an unusually long time and went to investigate. She found Dad slumped over the snowplow. He had obviously had a heart attack. My brothers were someplace hauling timber with the truck, so in desperation she had come to get us girls.

When we got to where Dad and the horses were, my sister unhitched the team from the snowplow and took them to the barn. Mom and I took our toboggan and went back out to get my dad. At a time like this, it seems like a person gets stronger than one usually is. I was 14 years old at that time.

My mom, the nurse, another gal and I lifted Dad up and laid him on the toboggan. The nurse checked his pulse and informed us that he was gone. We covered him up with a quilt, took him back to the house and carried him into the folks' bedroom and laid him on the bed. We waited until my brothers came home and then they took over. They drove into town and saw to it that the proper legal procedures were followed, the funeral arrangements made, etc.

Dad died Dec. 9, 1929. His passing bothered me deeply for a long time afterward. I didn't feel like going back to school, so Mom let me stay home for a week. Then she insisted that I return to my classes so as not to get too far behind in my studies.

I attended the school at Buck Lake through my seventh grade. By then, Edgar and I were going together as good friends. I decided to go back to Daybrook School for my eighth grade. There were only five kids in school at that time and I had a good teacher.

This teacher always had me do lots of drawing for her and I loved it—not only because I liked to draw, but possibly because I sensed that doing this for her frequently helped keep me in her good graces. I wasn't aware at that time that there was such a thing as a natural-born artist, or that and I was one of them. Peabrain that I was at the time, I was totally ignorant of the fact that I had been gifted with an invaluable talent and one that I was destined to make good use of later in my life. As I look back to that time, I still harbor a mild resentment against that teacher because she was aware that I possessed this potential but did not see fit to so inform me, for some reason.

I always got along well with the other kids in school. I attribute this to the fact that I was inclined to be somewhat shy, quiet, bashful and timid. I would go along with whatever the other kids wanted to do.

At this school, it was a custom for one student to take the responsibility of seeing to it that a fire was started in the heating stove before school started. It was sort of on a volunteer basis and whoever had the job got paid $5 for doing this for one month. We all took turns doing this for one month at a time. We were expected to come to the schoolhouse early, so as to have the schoolroom warming up pretty well by the time the teacher and the rest of the students got there. Of course, I took my turn at doing this as often as I could because I needed the $5.

EDGAR & ALLIE, MARCH 21, 1935

7

For better, for worse

After I graduated from the eighth grade, I decided I wanted to go on to high school. Everyone who lived in District One and wished to go beyond eighth grade had to attend the high school in Grand Rapids, about 35 miles southwest of our place. Arrangements were made for me to stay with a family in Grand Rapids and work for my board and room during the school term. There were tasks to be performed before I left for school and tasks awaiting me when I got home in the evening, so I didn't have too much time for socializing.

Back in those days, the town kids sort of looked down on us country kids. They didn't try to conceal the fact that they thought they were a little better than us "hayseeds." So I pretty much sought my companionship with other kids who were from rural areas like myself.

I went through the ninth grade and decided not to go on through the next three grades. I didn't enjoy going to that school very much. It was too far from home. I couldn't get home on weekends unless my brother would come and get me. Too, the distance separating me from Edgar was too great and the opportunity to spend time with him was too sparse to suit me!

My brothers got out of the logging business after Dad passed away. My younger brother, Auno, sort of took over the financial responsibilities at home, which took a heavy load off of my mother. He worked for the county whenever work was available, which paid fairly well. Auno was a good trapper and that provided extra income, also. In due time, he earned enough spare money to buy himself a car.

Auno was a good dancer and he would frequently ask me if I would like to go with him to the Saturday night dance. Of course, this was always fine with me, but there was a catch to it...I had to wash his white cotton shirt and iron it and also press his trousers. This was fine with me, as I welcomed the opportunity to go to the dance.

Things commenced changing around home. My brothers came and went as they well-pleased now that Dad was gone. We girls were younger and had to get our work done before we could go and visit our friends at Buck Lake; and when we did go, we had to get back in time to do the chores.

Lots of young folks visited our place, especially in the wintertime. We had those big, high hills around our place and a long toboggan that would hold quite a few of us at a time. We'd be out there sliding downhill on the new snow half of the night. The boys always pulled the toboggan back up the hill for us girls and away we'd go again, sailin' down that old hill a'heck a'hoppin'!

Finally, when we were getting tired, we would traipse back to the house, our clothes wet and covered with snow. We would scatter the wet, snowy clothes all over my mom's kitchen floor to dry out a bit. Mom didn't mind. She was always glad to see us kids having a good time. "We can always mop up the water," she would say with a smile.

The young folks in our community, many families of us, never went so far as to fall in love. We were all just good friends with one another. As time went on and more young adults were able to buy automobiles, changes began taking place amongst our peer group. Everyone started traveling a bit farther away from the immediate community, going to dances farther away and doing different things. Seemed like everyone went separate ways.

People sort of quit visiting as they used to. Everyone seemed to be busy with other more important things. Boys got girlfriends and girls got boyfriends. More and more of them got jobs and working took more of their time. Lots of my old friends moved into town, or even to another state in some instances.

I got a job working in Hibbing, which caused some problems between Edgar and me, but we finally got things worked out and got back together again. Later, when Edgar and I got married, lots of folks said that it wouldn't last; that it wouldn't work out. We were married on March 21, 1935, and 57 years later, we're still proving all those crepe-hangers to be wrong.

We named our daughter, and only child,

Marjorie Jean, when she joined the roster of the Brooks family. From early on, she was a joy to both Edgar and me, and still is to this very day. Both her dad and her mother find little cause to deny that her ongoing presence in our lives may well have been the bonding agent that has kept our union intact.

We lived with Edgar's parents when we were first married, until we got our own house built. The house was just a shell, but we were happy to have our own place in which to live. When the trapping season was open, Edgar made enough money selling his pelts to buy us a wood-burning cookstove. Edgar's folks gave us enough furniture and dishes from their place for us to get by nicely. Neither of us had been used to fancy surroundings while we were growing up, so we were able to get by with what we had and be satisfied with it.

In the wintertime, the house wasn't too warm. We could keep it warm all right during the daytime by keeping a hearty wood fire going in the stove. But when we would wake up in the morning the house would be nearly as cold on the inside as it was outside. Our drinking water pail would have ice an inch thick on top of the water and we'd have to punch a hole through the ice to get water for coffee and washing our faces.

Mom had made Edgar and me a wool quilt that kept us warm at night, even during the coldest weather; and when Marjorie was little, Mom made one just like it for her. This quilt, her very own, was Marjorie's pride and joy!

We built a barn as soon as we could after we got our house built, and eventually acquired some cattle and a flock of laying hens. When we got enough money together, Edgar bought a team of horses, which we used for hauling in

wood from out in the timber that literally surrounded our place. Edgar also used the horses
during haying time and for pulling an old walking plow that he had picked up at a farm sale
somewhere to plow our garden in early summer.

We raised raspberries and strawberries, and
picked blueberries that grew wild most everywhere for our fruit. We had a big garden that
provided us with our vegetables, including scads
of potatoes. I canned stuff all summer long.
Some folks find it difficult to believe it when I
tell them that we often were able to get by on as
little as $5 during a whole month for store-
bought groceries. All we had to buy was flour,
coffee and sugar.

When we were running short of meat, we
would butcher a pig, which provided us with
enough fat to render into lard to carry us for
quite a spell. Once a year or so, Edgar would
butcher a young beef, which seemed to be a special treat over and above our more usual diet of
pork. During deer season, we had fresh venison
readily available. So, you see, we were able to
get along nicely without requiring a large
amount of cash. We cooked simple meals—meat,
potatoes and vegetables—and once in awhile I'd
bake a cake or a pie or a batch of cookies, which
always seemed to disappear in a hurry, especially when little Marjorie got big enough to sneak
into our little pantry and help herself to those
"off-limits" goodies!

Somewhere along the line, we started taking
in hunters during deer hunting season. Edgar
soon built up a good reputation as a guide and
people would come from as far as the Twin
Cities to hunt at our place. They would stay at
our place and I would cook their meals for them.

One time when I was cooking a meal for our

hunting guests, Marjorie asked, "Mama, when we get rich, can we buy some bananas?"

I said, "Yes, dear, we'll buy some bananas when we get rich."

I chanced to repeat to our group what Marjorie had said and whenever they had occasion to come to our place after that, they would always bring Marjorie a supply of candy and fruit, including bananas.

Sometimes they would bring lots of clothes that I could make over for her or for myself. My mom had a sewing machine, so I had learned how to sew quite well; but when I got married, I didn't have one of my own, so I sewed Marjorie's by hand.

Eventually, I was able to scrape enough money together to buy myself a sewing machine. I put it to good use making sheets, pillowcases and dish towels from those old flour sacks that most everyone accumulated in goodly numbers back then. I made all of Marjorie's clothes, as well as most of my own, for many years. I still sew a lot.

When Marjorie was about three and one-half years old, she contracted whooping cough. From this, she developed a mastoid that had to be operated on. She came through the surgery all right, but the inner wall of her ear collapsed, so she doesn't hear well with that ear. Today, all this could have been averted with antibiotics, but this treatment was unheard of then.

When Marjorie was about five years old, she came down with scarlet fever and that came as quite a blow to us. Someone from the Health Department came and put a quarantine sign on our door warning anyone who might come to our place not to come near the house and also forbidding us to venture off of our own premises.

Our little daughter was quite ill with the fever at first, but soon broke out in a heavy rash and then began to respond favorably to her medication and to our tender loving care. Next, I came down with it, which meant an unwelcomed extension to our quarantine!

As soon as my mom heard about our dilemma, she came bustling over to deliver a quart of whiskey with slivered camphor in it. She wouldn't give any of this concoction to me because I was already down with the scarlet fever, but she induced my brother and Edgar to drink it. I don't know how much she gave them, but in any event, neither of them got the fever, and they were both right there in the house around me all the time.

I was so sick during my siege with the fever that I didn't care whether I lived or not. I had such a high temperature that my tongue, mouth and throat were all blisters. I wasn't breaking out with the pimply rash, as Marjorie had done. I was literally on my death bed and didn't know it.

Edgar's mother came over every day to take care of Marjorie and me. She made me some custard, but I had a difficult time swallowing it. I was encountering trouble drinking water, also. The next day, she brought me some ice cream. I ate about a tablespoon or two of it and that seemed to do the trick! Wonder of wonders, I broke out with a rash almost immediately, the fever broke and I started to get better.

I wasn't left with any adverse aftereffects, but Marjorie wasn't so fortunate. She got rheumatic fever and had to stay in bed for six weeks. She had black and blue spots all over her legs, as though someone had beaten her badly. The doctor told us to keep her in bed until those spots were gone.

I spent most of my time with her because she felt good and wanted to get up and play ever so badly. She didn't understand why she was being kept in bed all the time and told not to move around any more than was absolutely necessary. I read lots of stories to her and let her draw pictures and color them to keep her mind occupied. I was really relieved when that six weeks was over and those spots were all gone! But now she had to learn to walk all over again.

There are many episodes that I could include in this resumé of my life, but I will dispense with them, since Edgar will be including most of them in his story.

My mother passed away April 9, 1952. By this time, we had sold our farm and moved to a resort on Napoleon Lake that Edgar and I purchased and operated for a number of years.

Writing this synopsis of the highlights of my life has revived many ancient memories that are very precious to me. As I write this, my younger brother, Auno, is in the Leisure Hills Nursing Home. My sister, Aili, lives in Virginia, Minnesota, and I am still here at Buck Lake with Edgar.

A
Consuming
Habit

8

First homestead

(As told by Edgar Brooks)

When we began to build our house on the 160 acres my folks gave Allie and me at the time of our marriage, we got a man by the name of "Chicago Bum" from Nashwauk to help build the basement. He was a stone mason by trade; he also liked his whiskey.

The whiskey didn't seem to affect his work adversely, for I never saw a man work any harder than "Chicago" did in all my life. He pretty near killed me off buildin' that stone basement! I was mixing the mortar and hauling rocks and he was laying them up. It took us about 15 days to complete the job as I recall.

I paid him $3 a day, which was the wage he

103

had stipulated when I hired him. After we had put the finishing touches on the job, I paid him $45 and drove him back to Nashwauk.

When we got to town, "Chicago" and I walked into a pool hall that served beer and a little hard liquor on the side. As soon as we entered the place, "Chicago" threw both arms in the air, high over his head, and yelled, "Timber!" at the top of his voice for all to hear. He blew the entire 45 bucks on drinks for the crowd in that place, right while I was there! My basement was built and his money was gone.

When Marjorie was old enough, she began to attend the same school that I attended as a boy. My dad was driving the school bus at that time, and he would come by and pick her up, along with the other children on his route, and take her to grade school.

Later, after we had sold our farm and moved up onto our resort property on Napoleon Lake, it became necessary for our daughter to stay with some people we knew in Nashwauk in order for her to continue her schooling. She went all through high school there. Following her graduation from high school, Marjorie attended a business college in Minneapolis. This enabled her to get a job doing office work in Minneapolis. This experience served all of us in good stead when we went into the taxidermy business some years later in Minneapolis. The knowledge she had acquired in bookkeeping, typing and how to conduct business in general, proved to be a key factor in the remarkable success we experienced during those years we were in the taxidermy business.

ROLLER SKATING

While we were still on the farm, an incident

occurred that was to have serious consequences. A roller skating rink came into Hibbing
and Allie and I would pick up a small gang of
friends and go skating there quite often.

One night while we were skating, some big
dude collided with Allie and knocked her down,
injuring her back. This didn't seem to be a serious thing at the time but in due time, ramifications developed from this incident that was to
have a profound affect on both our lives and
Marjorie's, too, for that matter. More about this
a little later.

MORE THAN A PET

When Marjorie was small, Allie and I both
thought she was about the cutest little girl that
God ever put on this earth. We had a big shep-
herd dog that she played with almost constantly
when she was home.

About an hour or so before it came time for
my father to bring Marjorie home from grade
school on the school bus, our dog would trot
down the road to the place he knew she would
get off the bus. That dog would wait patiently,
right there in that spot, until she arrived. Then
they would come romping home together. That
dog thought the world of that little girl!

When they would get to the house, the dog
would crawl into his doghouse and pretend to
hide from Marjorie. Then she would get ahold of
the dog's chain and begin shaking it vigorously.
When she did that, the dog would commence
howling and snortin' and growling, and act like
he was going to bite her in half, but no way
would that dog harm a single hair of her head;
not for all the rice in China.

All the while we lived on the farm, we heated

the house with wood. The first year we were there, we failed to get our winter's supply of wood in on time. So I said to Allie, "There's one thing we can do. We'll teach this dog to pull our sled and I'll stay out there in the woods where I'm doin' the cuttin' and send the dog back to the house loaded with wood. You can unload the wood and send him back out to me for the next load. That's how we'll get our supply of wood hauled in." And that is exactly what we did.

We trained the dog to pull the sled and it took only a surprisingly short time for him to catch onto the routine that he was to follow. At times, he would stop in the middle of the homeward trip and take a short rest. Then he would continue on home, where Allie would be waiting to unload the sled. Then, back he'd come, proud as punch of his role in this unique operation and we would repeat the performance all over again.

When I would have occasion to go hunting, he would accompany me out into the woods. I would sit down on a stump and turn him loose on his own. Pretty soon, he would have a deer heading my way. How he always managed to drive those deer to a point within shooting range, I'll never know, but I'll have to say one thing for him, he sure did know his business when it came to deer huntin'.

If I crippled a deer, if I drew blood on it when I shot it, I didn't have to worry about it. That dog would get on his trail and eventually lead me to it. He had a special way of barking that would let me know he had a deer backed up against a windfall or something and had him at bay.

I guess it doesn't take much in the way of imagination to relate to the fact that a family pet that served in the triple capacity of a pet, a

domestic servant and a hunting dog, really got under our skin.

We discovered when winter set in for real that ours was not the warmest house in the world. We had built it in a hurry and it still wasn't quite finished. On some of those cold mornings, the water pail would be frozen.

We heated the house with a type of barrel stove that had become quite popular in our area at the time. I think some teacher over in Hibbing came up with the idea and it sort of caught on in these parts. This heating stove consisted of two barrels positioned horizontally. The bottom barrel had metal legs welded to it to keep it about 12 inches, maybe 18, off the floor. The second barrel was separated from the lower with metal strap-iron braces. At one end of the bottom barrel, a short piece of metal stovepipe permitted the smoke and heat from the fire in the bottom barrel to flow upward into the upper barrel, which served as a secondary heating chamber. A metal stovepipe going upward through the ceiling and outside the roof of the house was connected to the opposite end of the upper barrel from the end where the short stovepipe was situated.

A commercially-built metal door with latch and hinges was welded or bolted to the front end of the lower unit. Built into this door was a device that could be slid one way or the other to create more or less draft for the fire, as desired. This was somewhat of a crude arrangement by today's standards, but was actually quite efficient. The secret of its success was attributable to that secondary heating chamber that the upper horizontal barrel provided.

Now, anyone who has been around wood burning stoves to any extent, knows full-well how creosote can accumulate in the chimney and present a fire hazard if not cleaned out periodically. More than once, we've gotten up in the morning, started the fire in the barrel furnace, opened the draft and let'er rip; then discovered that creosote in the chimney had gotten red hot and was spewing onto the roof and sometimes on the upstairs ceiling in the house through loose joints in the metal chimney! Then, we'd have to run and fetch water in pails to pour on the small chunks of hot creosote that were threatening to burn the house down.

One time, I came home late in the evening; I had been out loggin' in the timber and my feet were wet. I was wearing a pair of real nice wool socks Allie had knitted for me. The fire had burned down in our barrel heating stove to the extent that the upper heating chamber was nicely comfortable to the touch. So, I removed my wet socks and placed them on that upper barrel to dry them out. I soon forgot about them and went to bed with those wet socks still on the stove.

The following morning I got up, tossed some wood into that ol' stove, lit the fire, opened the draft full on and went on about some timely tasks around the place. Well, to make this story short, my favorite pair of knit wool socks burned up! I guess I don't have to tell you that's the last pair of wool socks Allie ever knitted for me! I never figured out just why she got so mad about it, but I recall her sayin' to me, "No more wools socks for you, boy!"

One day, I was working out in the field and my brother returned home from fishing. He had picked up a small fawn and had carried it home in his arms. I don't recall exactly under what circumstances he happened onto it out in the woods, but he apparently thought Marjorie, our little daughter, might enjoy having it as a pet.

My brother was right in this assumption, for Marjorie immediately fell in love with that baby deer. Now, we reasoned, we had to figure out a way to get the dog to accept this newcomer to the family. This was eventually accomplished and it became really heartwarming to observe those three playing together.

After the fawn had grown a little, it learned to jump the yard fence without any tutoring. Sometimes it would jump back and forth over the fence several times in succession as a sort of game it was enjoying. Of course, Marjorie and

the dog would have to go around by the gate when they wanted through, while the fawn took the short-cut. Then it would prance and strut its stuff until they arrived.

Sometimes that fawn, whom we named Babe, would wander away from the immediate area around our house and the out buildings, but Shep always knew where Babe was. Now, how our dog knew where that deer might have gone was always a mystery to me. If company happened to drop in on us and we wanted to show them our pet deer, all we had to say was, "Go get Babe," and that dog would give one sharp bark and head for the woods beyond our pasture like a streak of lightening! Sometimes, he'd be gone for a half-hour or so, but pretty soon, here they'd come back together and everything was back in order again.

Things weren't always a bed of roses around our place, let me assure you. There were occasions a'plenty that gave us cause for concern. During the winter months, we watered our cattle down in the Daybrook River. I would cut a hole in the ice, whenever it was necessary, so the cattle could drink.

Allie and I were sittin' in the house one day and here came Marjorie soakin' wet from head to toe. She had traipsed down to the river and fallen into the water through that hole I had made for the livestock. We wondered how she could have gotten out of the water by herself. But when ol' Shep showed up about then, shaking water out of his long body hair all over the place, we had our answer. That dog was a godsend for us in so many ways. I couldn't ever begin to enumerate them all. He was one wonderful dog.

Shep got to be awfully good with the cattle, too. We had a pretty big pasture on our quarter-section of land and when milking time came around, he would take it upon himself to go out and bring the cows in, right up to our gate. Dad's cows and ours pastured together some of the time and during those occasions, Shep would separate Dad's from ours without any help on our part and send them in the direction of the folks' place, which lay between our homestead and the highway to the east of us.

There was one little exception to his emerald performance as a cow dog. If it was rainin' and thunderin', with lightening flashing across the sky, Edgar would have to get into his raincoat and go after them in person, because that darned dog would absolutely refuse to go out after those cows in a bad storm!

HUNTING LEGEND

Eventually, I got around to putting up a wind charger to charge the batteries for electric lights in the house and the barn. It stood on four legs that tapered up to the top from a wider base at the bottom. This structure made an ideal place for the hunters who came to our place during deer hunting season to hang carcasses.

By this time, I had gotten into the business of hiring on as a guide for hunters—usually up from the Twin Cities—which paid very well during deer hunting season. We would provide them a place to bunk in for the night while they were with us. Allie cooked the meals for them and they would slip her some extra money for that.

It was common practice for these fellows to bring the deer they shot up to the house and hang the carcasses up in the tower of our wind charger. Nuthin' to it...with one exception: It was all right for them to hang the deer up in that tower, but if anyone tried to go back there

to retrieve their game, or even to take a good look at it, they had ol' Shep to contend with! No way was anyone going to tamper with hanging carcasses while he was anywhere around. If I was present, then it was O.K. Otherwise, no deal.

At that time, Allie and I didn't realize the integral part our relationship with at least some of these hunters would one day play in our lives. Little could we imagine the undreamed of proportions we were destined to reach in a business that we would be getting into some years down the road. But that is another story in itself, which will be shared with you a bit later.

When we were young—and a bit foolish, I'll have to admit—some of my buddies and I would sometimes take it upon ourselves to open up our own private deer hunting season. We couldn't afford to indulge in some of the more expensive forms of exciting entertainment available to some of the richer kids in town. So, us guys out around Buck Lake would get our kicks by teasing the game wardens. Several rather exciting episodes took place that I can laugh about now, when viewed in retrospect. Some of them weren't all that funny at the time, however.

One evening, Allie was cooking up some fresh, out-of-season venison on the stove when a great big car drove into our yard! Well, I ran into the kitchen, grabbed the meat off the stove and headed for the woods with it, thinking that it was the game warden. However, after I had hastily disposed of what was to have been the good part of our supper, this guy turned out to be someone our four-year-old, Marjorie, knew.

Only after I had returned to the house empty-handed—and by this time, Shep was havin' himself a feast on what was to have been our supper—did I learn that our unexpected visitor wasn't an officer of the law, but was the manual training teacher at the Chisholm school.

When he knocked on the door, Marjorie answered it and he said, "Where's your dad?"

"Oh!" Marjorie replied, "He went that way with the meat." Well, he never did let me forget that episode!

LUMBERJACK

We used to have a lot of company from Iowa. On one occasion, Marion Robinson and his wife, Betty, who is my cousin, came up for a visit. They spent a few days with us and before they got ready to go home, Marion asked me if it might be possible for him to come up here to do some trapping with me later in the fall. "Great," I said, "come on up."

That fall, Marion came up and he and I went out and bought an old Model A Ford and went trappin'. Now, Marion decided to let his whiskers grow while he was there so that when he went back home to Betty, he'd look like a regular lumberjack, y'know.

Everything went along just fine and we trapped together for a month or so. By this time, the trapping season was pretty well over and deer season was about to open. So, Marion and I and another fellow went up to Grass Lake to do some hunting. We tramped the woods all day long and were really pooped when night came around.

We came into camp, built ourselves a fire, made some coffee and lunch and got ready to go to bed. We cut some balsam boughs and put them on the ground to lay on. I rolled up my jacket for a pillow, but Marion proceeded to make his pillow out of some birch bark he found and rolled up for that purpose. Then, we all stretched out on the ground and went to sleep.

Sometime during the night, I was awakened by the damndest roar you ever heard! I couldn't imagine what was the matter. I was so sleepy that I couldn't remember where I had laid my rifle if it was a bear.

Only after I got fully awake and got my senses together a bit better, did I realize what the commotion was all about. A spark had flown out of the bonfire and landed on Marion's birch-bark pillow. When it did, that roll of birch bark ignited and really commenced burning in earnest and Marion's prized growth of whiskers got singed off out of the deal! While this was happening, Marion was yellin' and jumping around something fierce. He looked for all the world like a human sparkler!

114

Booze 'n Butte

We had built up a rather sizable herd of cattle and things were looking pretty good for Allie and me and Marjorie there on the farm. Then a recession set in and all of a sudden, things took a turn toward more skimpy times around there.

We heard that the mining companies up around Butte, Montana, were hiring laborers to work underground in the mines and we made inquiries that substantiated this information. So, Allie and I talked it over and decided we would go and seek our fortune out there at Butte.

We made arrangements to distribute our cattle around amongst some of our neighbors and got somebody to occupy our farm. Then, we packed up some personal belongings and drove out to Montana. Looking back on this decision now, I think this was one of the biggest mistakes I ever made. Butte, Montana was no place for anyone inclined to drink alcohol. The bars were open 24 hours a day and were patronized well all the while.

Now, when we went to work in those underground mines, we were down there for an eight or ten-hour shift. When we came topside, we could go into any one of 30 or 40 bars in town, plunk our dinner pails on the bar and they would serve us boilermakers right then and there. Now, friends, this isn't a good circumstance for a person who has a problem with alcohol.

If you wanted to be a big shot, you could buy your drink and for every ten-cent beer you bought, they would give you a shot of whiskey. All of these places were full of gambling devices of every description. They had card tables, slot machines, roulette games and just about every other kind of gambling facility you could imagine. The quicker they could get you drunk, the quicker they could get your money away from you and then kick your butt out of there to fare for yourself as best you could.

I worked in the mines at Butte for quite some time and my problem with alcohol progressed from bad to worse, which wasn't helping our situation any around home, believe me. Along about this time, World War II broke out.

When the Japanese bombed Pearl Harbor on Dec. 7, 1941, this traumatic, historic event not only changed the traditional manner in which these mines were operated, it suddenly brought about a drastic right-about-face for nearly every man, woman and child in the entire United States of America, almost overnight.

Suddenly, large industrial companies were confronted with problems they had given little or no thought to prior to Pearl Harbor. One of these concerns was the possibility of sabotage. So it was that the mining company I was working for decided to take an extra precaution to lessen chances of foreign agents, sympathetic to the cause of our enemies, slipping in and blowing up the powder magazines, an important aspect of the overall mining operation.

After several behind-closed-door meetings on the part of the company's big shots, it was decided that they would "stucco" these containers of explosives in order to protect them from sabotage. A wet mixture of sand and cement called Gunite was sprayed, under extremely high pressure, over the explosives to form a protective coating. Gunite could even be used, and was, by some large house-building contractors to apply an exterior coating of stucco-like substance on frame buildings.

Well, anyway, the shift boss came to me one

day and said, "Edgar, can you run a Gunite machine?"

"Sure," I said. "Of course, I can run a Gunite machine; what is it?"

"Edgar," he responded, "that's a pretty good attitude. I'll show you what a Gunite machine is and how it works."

So they put me on that Gunite machine and I worked in that capacity for several weeks. But, in view of things in general, Allie and I decided it might be best for us to call it quits in Butte and head back home to Minnesota. The war was on now and we felt it wise to go home and get our cattle gathered back together to our place and get to farming once more. In less time than it takes to tell it, we were packed up and headed back east.

WILD RICE

The people whom we had left in charge of our farm back home were adept at picking wild rice and we arrived back at our farm just at the time the ricing season was in full swing. This fellow asked us if we had ever picked wild rice and we informed him that we hadn't. He volunteered to teach us how it was done and assured us that we would enjoy doing it. This man's name was Albert Newman. His wife's name was Stella. Their suggestion was so impressive that Allie and I decided to give it a whirl.

Albert and his wife accompanied us over to a nearby lake where we were to get our instructions as to how this operation was done. They had their boat and as I recall, Allie and I used our canoe. The procedure wasn't overly difficult to learn and in a short time, Allie and I were getting enthusiastically oriented into this new adventure.

The routine was relatively simple. One of us would propel the boat by the use of a long pole. When the boat had been poled into a wild rice paddy, the second person in the boat used two wooden sticks to bend the rice plants over the gunnel of the boat, or in our case the canoe, and beat the wild rice grain off the stem into the boat. The term for this aspect of the operation was "knocking rice." The instrument with which the boat was maneuvered from place to place in the lake was called a rice pole.

Well, things went pretty well for us in this new venture and we made some pretty good money. Eventually, we enlarged on our ricing operation by buying a truck and hauling six or eight boats, manned by hired help, to locations we knew abounded with wild rice paddies.

We worked out an arrangement with these rice pickers whereby I bought the rice they had harvested each day for so much a pound. I had entered into a contract with a company in Cohasset, Minnesota, which purchased our harvest of rice for around 25 cents a pound. Within a year or two's time, we were getting more than a dollar a pound. With this increase in the price of wild rice, more people got into the business than had been the case in the early days of our ricing business.

I recall one of the last times we picked rice. We went on the Vermilion River with nine boats and the crew to man them. There was a stretch of about nine miles between the waterfalls where wild rice grew thick. Allie and I would thresh about 200 pounds of rice into our canoe, then go in and have dinner. After dinner, we would go back out and pick another several hundred pound boatload before coming in for supper. Then we would call it a day.

Nine boats. Beautiful! Over $100 a day—and that was good wages in those times. But the last time we went up there to harvest wild rice, there were 70 boats in the area we had intended working. We took one brief look at the situation and went back home without even unloading our boats. Soon after that, we sold our ricing equipment and went out of the business. I guess our timing was just about right, for the wild ricing business sort of went kaput soon after that.

GONE FISHIN'

Along about this time, Allie and I decided to take off a few days and go up to Napoleon Lake to do some fishing and man, did we catch fish! I had never seen such fishing in my life before then, or after. The fish seemed to be laying just under the surface of the water, despite the fact that it was a scorching hot day when fish normally seek deeper waters where the water temperature is cooler.

We kept only what we wanted to eat and put the rest back. We fished all day and it was getting dark by the time we finished eating our supper, cooked over an open wood fire on the lakeshore. Then after supper, Allie and I crawled into our Chevy coupe and went to sleep.

We hadn't been asleep very long when the sound of an airplane woke us up. Looking up, we could see a bright, square light shining from the underbelly of the plane that was flying over the lake in our direction. We watched as it passed overhead and disappeared into the night beyond us. Then, Allie and I got back into our car to try to get back to sleep. Suddenly, we heard a man's voice screaming and it sounded

like it was coming from out in the lake somewhere.

We couldn't figure what in the world was
going on. This sort of thing just didn't occur in
this part of the country, y'know. So, I had Allie
take the gun and step back into the brush near
the car.

I could tell that the guy who was doing the
hollering was out there in the lake someplace,
so I climbed up on top of the car with my flashlight and yelled back, "What in the world is the
matter?"

"I bailed out of that airplane," the voice
answered. "Can you direct me to shore?"

I was able to direct him to shore in fairly
short order and we then learned that he had
parachuted from the plane and, fortunately for
him, had landed in rather shallow water. He had
been able to get unbuckled from his chute and
remove his water-filled boots before making his
way up out of the lake.

When he approached me, I noticed that his
breath smelled strongly of gasoline. "What in the
world happened?" I inquired of him.

"We left Texas on a test flight," he replied.
"We were supposed to fly up through this country, then fly back to Texas. Our airplane started
to gassing badly in the cab and we couldn't
determine just what was causing it. It got so
bad in there that we knew there was nothing
else to do but bail out and take our chances on
making a reasonably safe landing in the dark-
ness.

"We put the plane on automatic pilot and
made arrangements to abandon ship, in a manner of speaking. Two of the guys jumped ahead
of me, I was the third to leave. There were nine

of us all together and we were jumping out about four miles apart."

At first, Allie and I were in somewhat of a quandary as to what to do next. We finally decided to drive our unexpected visitor over to the nearest fire ranger station. We woke up the ranger and explained to him what had happened. The proper authorities were notified and Allie and I returned to Napoleon Lake, leaving the ranger in charge of the stranger.

We fished the following morning and then headed for home right after lunch. About four miles from where we had been camping on the lake, we spotted a man walking out of the brush and onto the road ahead of us. It turned out to be the fellow who had bailed out of the airplane just ahead of the man we had helped rescue the night before.

"I knew there was no use for me to start out for anywhere," he volunteered. "When I hit the ground and found out that I wasn't hurt, I just rolled up in my parachute and went to sleep. I figured when the sun came up, I'd have a better chance of getting my bearings."

We picked this fellow up and drove him back to the fire warden's station. Then, we went on home. Later, we learned that the first flyer had landed in a tall pine tree alongside a logging camp. He was hung up in his parachute way up in the top of that tree. So what did the loggers do? They came out with a chain saw and cut the tree down! The fellow wasn't hurt in the first place, but now they had broken his leg—put him in bad shape. We didn't find out what happened to the rest of that unfortunate crew, at least not until some time later; but we did hear that the plane finally crashed quite a long distance from our area.

Several years later, the fellow we rescued

dropped in to visit us. He was married by this time and he had his wife along with him. He wanted to show her exactly where he had landed out there in the dark of night, so we got in one of our boats and I took them out to the spot from which I had heard him yelling for help.

Allie had a nice meal prepared when we got back around noon and our visitors accepted her invitation to eat with us. They departed soon after we had eaten and we have never heard from them since.

NEW YEAR'S EVE

Along about this time, a fellow arrived in our area from Seattle, Washington. He was recruiting laborers for the Bremerton Shipyards. Well, we hadn't exactly succeeded in making our fortune in Butte, so we thought maybe going to work in the shipyards might be a good idea.

Allie and I packed up some of our belongings, distributed our cattle all around amongst some neighbors again, got on the train and headed for Seattle and Bremerton. My folks had gone to Washington before we had and were already working there when we arrived. We rented a house in Bremerton before going down to the shipyards to look for jobs.

Allie landed a beautiful job right off the bat and soon after that, I landed a job in Ordinance, working on big ships. Everything went along just fine until New Year's Eve came along. Now, for reasons that I am sure you are well aware of by this time, I've always had trouble gettin' past New Year's. It has never been a good day for me and this particular one was no exception. I got on a big drunk and got in a fight with the ship boss, which wasn't a good idea at all.

The next morning, they called me into the office and said, "Brooks, we've got a new job for you. Now, bein's that you like to fight so well, we're going to send you to the Army. They're looking for people who like to fight."

There really wasn't much I could do about this new situation. I knew full-well that I had goofed another opportunity. I was instructed to go over to Seattle and take my examination, then report in with the draft board back home.

I went to Seattle and took my examination for the Army, then came back to Bremerton to get ready for the trip home. I went into the gasoline rationing office to get the gas stamps I would need for the long trip back to Minnesota. The girl in the office was a little reluctant to issue me the stamps, stating that they didn't issue gas ration stamps to just everybody.

"Well," I said, "this is just fine. The draft board in Grand Rapids, Minnesota, is looking for me to report to them for induction and..."

"Oh, now that's a different story," she replied. "If the draft board is looking for you, we'll see that you get some gas." So, I got in line to receive my gasoline stamps.

While waiting in this line of people to receive my gas ration stamps, something happened that I will never forget as long as I live. The news came over the loud speaker that Franklin Delano Roosevelt had passed away. Although it was well-known that President Roosevelt's health had been deteriorating for some time, his unexpected death hit the entire country with a traumatic impact. No other president, before or since, has ever been elected to that office four consecutive terms. It was during the second year of his fourth term of office that F.D.R.—as he was fondly called by one and all—was fatally stricken by a massive brain hemorrhage. The year was 1945.

Later that same year, Harry S. Truman, who succeeded F.D.R. to the presidency of the United States, was to be confronted with the grave decision to drop the A-bombs on Hiroshima and Nagasaki, Japan—an event that brought the war with Japan to a sudden halt and altered the direction of history drastically.

I got my gas stamps O.K. and returned to Minnesota to report to my local draft board. Just how to best explain to them what had happened back there in the shipyards was presenting me with a bit of a problem, but it turned out that they knew all about what had taken place. They knew more about it than I did, as a matter of fact.

"There is one thing I would appreciate your doing for me," I said to them. "Would you give me time to sell my cattle before I go to the Army?"

"What do you mean, cattle?" the man at the draft board asked.

"I've got 28 head of milk cows scattered around amongst the neighbors," I replied, "and I would like to sell them before..."

"You're a dairy farmer?" he exclaimed. "Now, I'll tell you what you're going to do; you go out there and get those 28 head of milk cows back on that farm and you stay there until the war is over." And that's just exactly what I did.

9

Last resort

The following year, Allie and I decided to get into something a little different—something a little more exciting. We would dispose of our farm and open up a summer resort on a lake up in the boondocks somewhere.

We followed through on this idea and in 1946, we sold our farm and moved to Napoleon Lake. We had found a spot to our liking, "so far back in the woods that the crows can't even find it." Then, too, there wouldn't be any problem with booze in an out-of-the-way place like this, I reasoned.

O boy! Was that a misconception if there ever was one! There's more booze around a summer resort than there is around Crab Orchard, Kentucky. The way you could tell how good a week you'd had in that business, was to what degree you had the shakes when it was over with. Sometimes, I was shakin' so bad by

Monday, I couldn't hit my hind end with both
hands in three fair trials...

Starting from Scratch

Having gone ahead with our plans to build
the resort up on Lake Napoleon, Allie and I now
found ourselves involved not only in a new business, but a business that neither of us knew
anything about in the first place. The hunting
and fishing aspect of operating the resort didn't
present much of a problem; both Allie and I had
done our share of that. It was the business end
of this new operation that we were a little green
at.

When we let it be known among our peer
group that we were going into the summer
resort business, their response was a negative
one for the most part. "It won't work," they said.
"You can't go clear up there into that wild country and start a thing like that."

Well, we were determined to make it work,
one way or another. True, it was wild country,
way out in the boondocks and a goodly distance
off the main highway. When we would hear a
car coming down the road toward our place, we
knew where it was a'goin'. There was no place
else for it to go but to our place or Wilson Lake.

The last 10 miles coming into our resort consisted of little except two ruts in the sod and
both sides of this "road" were lined with pines.
Once you got there, our resort was one beautiful
spot to behold and the water in Napoleon Lake
was as clear as crystal.

There was one building on our property when
we bought it. It had served as a lodge building
prior to this time, but Allie and I used it as our
home to start with. We knew that the first big

project confronting us, now that we were here, was to get cabins built.

I knew of a man within 15 or 20 miles of there who could be of great help to us in building those cabins if I could get him sobered up and keep him sober for the job. He was quite a guy to drink, but a good worker.

"Let's go talk to Harry and see if we can get him to help us build these cabins," I said to Allie one day. This was in the spring of the year and a bridge between Harry's place and ours had washed out. So, when we started down to get Harry, we had to take some planks with us and construct a temporary, make-shift bridge across a narrow little swamp creek.

We made it down to Harry's place O.K. and sure enough, he was tighter than a drum! I thought, "Well, that's all right. When we get him back to our place and get him sobered up, everything will be fine." So we started for home.

When we got to the creek where the bridge had washed out, I stopped the truck to make sure I was lined up properly with those planks I had laid down. Before I could stop him, Harry got out of the truck to see if he could help in any way. All of a sudden, I heard Allie hollerin' at the top of her voice! The tone of her voice scared me, as Allie doesn't get that excited over little things.

I looked all about us to try to determine what was the matter and finally spied the bottom portion of Harry's boots protruding upright out of the swamp water! His head was down under, stuck in the mud and his boots were stickin' straight up in the air!

Harry had been eating some soda crackers when he fell into the creek. When we finally succeeded in extricating his head out of that mud and got it above water, he gave one big blow and

127

the crackers spewed from his mouth all over the place. That was some sight to behold, I'll tell you, with his big old lumberjack boots stickin' up out of the creek and his head stuck down in the mud! But when we had gotten him out of his predicament and back into the truck, everything was O.K. and we took off for the lodge.

We had just enough money on hand to buy the materials we needed to build one little cabin down by the lake and we had them delivered and stacked up near the spot we had picked out. We decided we wanted the cabin situated on a cement slab, which we would mix and pour ourselves. We didn't have anything in the way of cement working tools, so I decided I would mix the concrete by hand with a hoe and pour it into the forms with the use of a wheelbarrow. This is what might be called "doing it the hard way," but it was the way we had to go, due to our limited finances.

When it came time to do the finish work on this concrete slab, we didn't have a finishing trowel and didn't really have the spare money to buy one, so I ended up using Allie's pancake turner for getting this job done. When we start-

ed out, we had practically nothing...and we still got most of it left.

After quite a struggle, we finally got one cabin built. It wasn't too long after its completion that we had a few people coming along who wanted to rent that cabin. We got a dock built as quickly as we could and bought three or four metal fishing boats. I also made several flat-bottom boats so we now had about eight boats.

The brush Caddie

While all this was taking place, our daughter, Marjorie, was going to school in Minneapolis and staying with a very nice family there.

We got a letter from Marjorie one day informing us that the folks she was living with, and three other people, were interested in coming up and staying at our resort for an outing of several days. In addition to the man of the house where she was staying (who wanted to come a day or so ahead of the others), there was an executive from Schmidt Brewing Company, another from Hamms Brewing Company and one from the Grain Belt Brewing Company, all in Minneapolis.

We wrote back confirming the reservation and he arrived on the agreed upon day. The following morning, after we had finished our breakfast, we decided that since the rest of the party wouldn't be arriving until that evening, we would go over to Squaw Lake and do some duck hunting.

When we arrived back at the resort after a day of hunting, Allie informed us that the Minneapolis bunch had arrived already. I inquired of her as to where they were. "Gosh," she replied, "I'm not sure, but I think they went partridge hunting." This was really what they had come up to do—hunt ducks and partridge.

"It's a pretty big country and there's no way we would have much of a chance finding them if we were to set out looking for them, so I guess all we can do is sit here and wait for them to return," I said.

We waited around there for a long time and finally, one of the three fellows arrived. I don't recall exactly which one of them it was but boy, he was steamed right to the eyeballs! Tighter than a coot!

"We've got our car stuck on a back road where we were partridge hunting," he informed us.

"Where is it?" I inquired of him.

"Oh, just up the road aways," he responded.

When he explained to me approximately where they were, I had a pretty good idea about where their car really was. Now this car was a brand new Cadillac convertible that had been purchased expressly for this trip.

The road I figured they were on was a back road that was plum full of tag-alder. A friend of mine by the name of Bob Sharp happened to be at our place at the time and he accompanied our first guest, myself and this drunk as we set out in my pick-up truck to find the indisposed hunters.

When we arrived at the back road I figured they had taken, we could tell that it was the one they had taken by the way the brush was bent down in on it. We left the pick-up on the road and proceeded to walk on back into the wilderness about a mile. We finally found the ill-fated Cadillac and the other two guys sittin' on the trunk lid with a quart of booze between them and I'll tell you, they were really celebrating their partridge hunting event!

One good look at the situation convinced me that there was no easy way that we were going to be able to get that car out of the predicament it was in. All that brush was compressed up against it and I knew if we headed that car out of there, we were going to tear it all to pieces.

"I really don't know just how we're going to get you out of this mess," I said to them.

"Well, I'll tell you what you do," one of them responded. "You just get me out of this mud hole and headed toward that road we took off of gettin' in here. I'll show you how to get this auto out of here."

So, that's what we did. We finally got him turned around and he took off with the rear wheels throwin' mud 20 feet in the air! When he reached the road, he had torn the grille completely off, the cloth top was badly torn and the paint job was ruined. Believe me, that car looked like a total wreck, but it was still running!

The Cadillac and its driver were waiting for us at the road when the rest of us arrived back there on foot. Several of us got in my truck and the others followed us back to the resort in the new convertible.

Allie prepared supper for the entire group and after everyone had eaten, we retired to the family room to make our plans for the following day. All during this time, these guys from Minneapolis were sippin' on their hard liquor. In due time, our guests decided to call it a day and turned in for the night.

The cabin they were renting, as was the case with the ones that Allie and I built later, had no electricity, no running water and no modern toilets. They were strictly minimal housekeeping facilities whose furnishings consisted of beds, dining table and chairs, and very little else.

Sometime during the night, one of these fellows had to go to the toilet. Still inebriated from the booze that had been consumed right up to the time he had gone to bed, this fellow was clawin' his way around the dark interior of the cabin when he finally found the clothes closet. One of the other gentlemen had stashed his hip boots in that closet with the tops rolled part way down. In his drunken stupor, this guy figured what he was feeling in the dark must be the john and therewith proceeded to empty his distressed bladder into those boots!

When everyone in the cabin was getting dressed the following morning and the owner of the preempted boots slid his feet into them, there was quite a commotion goin' on around there for awhile, I'll tell you!

I think it is assumed by most folks that it is people of lower estate who do their celebrating and carrying on with liquor like this, but from what I have observed during our years in the resort business and later on in the taxidermy business, the more affluent people are, the worse they perform when they get out away from home.

When our daughter, Marjorie, came up and I told her what had happened she said, "The last thing the wives told them when they left was to behave themselves when they got up here." I guess they must have had some inkling what might happen.

When all of the hunters had gotten dressed, they trooped over to our place for breakfast. They looked very pale and drug-out...all of them except Marjorie's landlord, who had drunk very little, if any. We attempted to do some partridge and duck hunting throughout the day, but they were just too sick to enjoy it. In spite of this, they kept right on nipping on their bottles!

We managed to bag a fairly good number of birds by the end of the day, and I think they stayed one more night before pulling out for home.

IT CAN'T BE DONE?

Our business was escalating right along, and it soon became evident that Allie's and my first priority was to get more cabins built. We did a lot of the work on this project ourselves and soon started feeling quite proud of our prowess as cabin builders—especially, in laying up the stone fireplaces that we put in some of them. Eventually, we wound up with five rental cabins. Still later, we put in a small combination grocery store and beer tavern to accommodate our customers. The fishing was exceptionally good on our lake during the spring and through the fall season. Deer were also plentiful in those days. Between these two valuable assets, our resort business was starting to flourish, despite the warnings that we had received at the outset to the affect that there was simply no way we could establish a resort so far back in the wilderness as this and make a go of it. Now that I look back, had Allie and I listened to all of these "advisors," we would never have left the farm.

One disadvantage we were confronted with was getting our mail. We had to travel six or seven miles to its nearest point of delivery. I decided to see if I couldn't get something done to have it brought closer to our place. Again, everyone I discussed this matter with expressed doubts that it could be done. So, I made up a petition and went around to everybody in that entire area and got them to sign it. I forget how many signers I got but in any event, we got our mail brought to within a mile and a half of the resort.

The lack of electricity was our main handicap but I was able to solve this problem, to a degree at least, by purchasing an old, second-hand light plant from a neighboring resort.

My wife, Allie, always made it a practice to do the washing on Mondays. Now, Monday wasn't always one of my best days, for reasons that I have mentioned earlier. We had this old, gasoline-powered Maytag washing machine that had a tendency to be a bit difficult to get started at times. You'd stomp on the foot-pedal starter mechanism a dozen times before the cussed thing would finally take off runnin'. Once you got it started, it did a good job of washing clothes.

Well, on this particular Monday morning, I noticed Allie attempting to get her washing machine started and I decided to lend her my assistance. I reached down to get ahold of the choke, but instead of getting the choke, I got ahold of the sparkplug. When I stomped down on the foot-pedal starter, a jolt of electricity from the coil that supplied the juice to the sparkplug shot through me like a bolt of lightening!

I think I left the ground and circled the lake twice before I came back down to earth! When I lit, I was directly in front of Allie. She looked me square in the eye and said, "Get outa' here! I'll get it started by myself!"

"Well, fair enough; that's a good idea..."

Later, when we eventually got the Rural Electric Association (R.E.A.) line in to the resort, we exchanged the gas engine on that Maytag for an electric motor. After that, there were no problems starting it.

HOT STOVE

As time went on up there at our resort on Napoleon Lake, our patronage continued to grow. Things were going along pretty well for Allie and me, although it was getting to where we needed more help. So one day, I decided to drive over to Swanson's Store at Bear River and see if they knew of anybody we could hire to help Allie with her workload.

I explained what I wanted and also informed them I was in the market for an oil burner. They couldn't help me with the matter, so I drove back to the resort. I guess we finally got someone to help Allie; I don't exactly recall who at the moment, but I think my niece, Garnette, came up from Iowa for awhile.

Deer season had just opened and we had a heavy run of business during the first five days of hunting. On the sixth day, Allie and I started out to take the money we had earned to the bank.

When we had gotten about five miles from the resort, we met a car whose occupant stopped us.

"Are you Brooks?" the lone occupant of the car inquired of us.

"Yes, I'm Brooks," I replied. I could see right off that this guy was sort of shifty-eyed; someone to be a little wary of.

"I hear you want to buy an oil burner," he continued. It turned out that he had been at Swanson's Store that time I had gone there. He didn't tell us that, just said he had heard we were in the market for an oil burner.

"We're breaking camp up at Deer Lake, and I've got an oil burner I would like to sell you," he informed us.

I looked at the oil burner he had with him and it was a dandy. He said he wanted $25 for it and it looked like it was well worth that much, without any doubt.

I didn't have that much cash with me since our receipts had all been in checks, so I told him that if he wanted to accompany us down as far as Buck Lake, I would cash a check at the store there and pay him.

"Would you like me to take the oil burner to your place?" the man countered. I didn't feel there was any good reason to do this, so we loaded the oil burner in our truck and went on down to the store at Buck Lake. I noticed that he signed his name "Zajack" when he endorsed the check in order to cash it there at the store.

Allie and I went on about our business at the bank in town and went back to the resort later in the day, quite well-pleased with our purchase of the oil burner we had been wanting.

A few weeks later, a couple of men from Iowa came to our place. They wanted to do some winter fishing. We put them up in the upstairs bedroom of our house for the night and Allie and I were sleeping in the living room downstairs.

All of a sudden, the front door smashed open. I could see flashlights shining in through the windows and I could see a badge on the fellow who had made the unannounced entrance into our home and was now standing by our temporary bed. There was another guy with him and I could see that the gun he held in his hand was just a'shakin'.

"Do you have some people staying here?" the officer asked.

"Yes, we have two people here. They're sleeping upstairs." When I said this, the guy with the gun really got nervous and his gun was shakin' all the more!

"They're from Iowa," I explained. "They're here to do some fishing."

"Did you buy an oil burner recently?" the officer asked. I informed him that we had and where we had gotten it.

"How did you pay for it?" he inquired further.

I told him, "By check."

"Do you know where he cashed the check?"

"Yes, down at the Buck Lake Store."

The officers then went upstairs to check out our two guests who were sleeping there. Then, the fellow in charge demanded that we go with them to the store to try to trace the check I had given the man when I bought the oil burner.

Now, this "Zajack," who sold us the stove, used about five different names. The name "Zajack" was an alias. He had started from Missouri on this last trip. He had a girl with him, whom they suspected he may have murdered somewhere along the way north.

When he got to Iowa, he had robbed a bank and took off, with the F.B.I. hot on his trail. He had killed both F.B.I. men when they were trying to apprehend him and then, he went on to Minnesota.

I would be willing to venture that this Mr. Zajack, or whatever his real name was, stole that oil burner out of a cabin somewhere to pick up some extra spending money. In any event, we read in the newspaper about six months later, where this guy had been shot over in Illinois. Officers of the law, including the F.B.I., finally caught up with him in a cornfield where he had taken refuge.

In looking back on this incident, it's a wonder that I didn't let him deliver the oil burner to our lodge at the resort as he suggested. Had I agreed to this, he would have cleaned us out, lock, stock and barrel, for sure.

The sheriff came by one day and confiscated the stove, so we didn't do too well on that deal, but it could have been worse. We felt we had been lucky in the overall, for we had been dealing with a pretty rough customer, by any standard that might be applied.

FIREPLACE

When Allie and I purchased the resort up on Lake Napoleon, a sizable area of land went with it. We decided, after we had gotten the resort built up and going good, that it might be a good idea to clear the trees off of some of this land and sell lots to people who wanted to build their own cabins in that area. Allie and I had acquired some experience in the building business by this time and could build these cabins on contract.

We went ahead with this plan and sold about 10 lots to people from various states outside Minnesota, as well as to some closer at hand. We then contracted with these folks to build their cabins, and most of them wanted fireplaces in them after looking at the ones Allie and I had built in our own cabins at the resort.

By the time we got these places built, there were others around the country wanting us to build for them. One party in the area had started building a large summer place and during the beginning stage of its construction, the man they had contracted to build it for them fell off a ladder injuring himself badly. Allie and I were contracted to take over the completion of the project.

We built a nice big cabin for these folks and laid up a nice stone fireplace in it. Mrs. Bond, the wife of the man I had made the deal with, was a bit on the ambitious side. She happened to notice we were getting some mortar on those stones as we went up with the fireplace.

"Edgar," Mrs. Bond asked me, "how do you get that stuff off of the stones?"

"With mercuric acid," I informed her. No more was said about it.

A couple of mornings later, I came to work and that whole fireplace was covered with foam—foam running down the mortar and out of the joints.

"What in the world has happened here?" I exclaimed!

"Well," she said, "I poured some of that acid on it. You said that's what you used for cleaning off the stones."

"My God, Mrs. Bond!" I exploded. "The directions are printed right there on the bottle. You have to add water to it first.

"When you have diluted the acid with water according to the directions, you carefully brush it on each stone, separately; you don't pour it over the entire fireplace at once," I informed her.

Allie and I had to redo the whole thing; started up from the bottom and rebuilt it from scratch a second time. It was quite a mess!

Mr. Bond's name was Beryl. When the situation Mrs. Bond had been instrumental in creating took place, I said to him, "Beryl, I think I'm going to give you this job."

"No," Beryl replied. "It'll be O.K. I've gotten into some bad situations myself. I am a metal

139

fabricator. One of the worst jobs I ever got tangled up in was making the campaign buttons for Thomas Dewey at the time he was running for election against Harry Truman in 1948. That didn't turn out too well. You may recall that on the night before the winner of the campaign for the presidency of the United States was to be announced officially, one of the largest newspapers in the country came out with a big headline to the affect that Tom Dewey, the Republican candidate, had won by a landslide. Imagine their embarrassment when Truman won the election, not Dewey. Their zealousness to get the jump on their competitors in the newspaper business backfired on them.

Allie and I finished building the cabin for Mr. and Mrs. Bond and it turned out to be a beautiful building, and we were quite proud of it.

Electricity

Now, one of the chief drawbacks in the operation of our resort was the lack of electricity. We had the little power plant that I bought early on, but it was limited in output capacity to merely taking care of some of our own needs at the lodge.

I went to the Rural Electric Association and inquired as to whether there was any chance we could get a line in to our resort and the surrounding vicinity. I was informed that they would have to take up the matter at a meeting of the board.

They discussed my inquiry at their next meeting and notified me that if I would come up to their office in Bigfork, the idea would be discussed further. I went up there and was told that if I could get a sufficient number of signers who would confirm they would hook up to the electricity, they would agree to run the line into our area.

There was one stickler to all this. The distance from the existing R.E.A. lines to our place was somewhere between six and seven miles, and one of the conditions of the agreement was that we had to clear the strip of land to make way for the poles upon which the line would be strung. Those of us who wanted electricity would have to cut down these trees ourselves.

That sounded fairly feasible, so I started going around to get the required signatures. I did all right getting those who wanted electricity to sign up, but when I came to the part about cutting down those trees to clear that long strip for putting in the poles, I ran into a snag. Not one of them would agree to help cut the trees!

I wanted this electricity run into our resort in the worst way, so I made a deal with everyone who had signed up. If each subscriber would pay us so much—and I don't remember exactly the amount we agreed upon—Allie and I would take the time to cut the trees. They all agreed to the plan and Allie and I tied into this project almost immediately. We worked at cutting down those trees all fall and halfway into the winter. Then, we decided to call a halt to the operation, leave the resort and go into Grand Rapids to live during the remainder of the winter.

I used my heavy-duty chain saw to cut down those trees and I could whack a tree down in nothin' flat when I really got into the swing of it. We might have hung in there and completed the job in one stretch, but Allie's old back injury was kicking up a fuss and I was about ready for a little time off from handling that heavy chain saw.

We stayed in Grand Rapids for about two months, then decided to get back to work on the project of cutting in that electric line. With all that time off to get rested up, I was really going to go back out there and tear things up! So we got out there, both of us put on our snowshoes and we went to work in earnest. That night, when we knocked off from the day's work, Allie just about had to wheel me back home. I had just about killed myself off!

In due time, we did manage to get the high line in. The paradox to all this is that in less than a year after we got the electricity, Allie and I sold the resort. We built a cabin right next to the resort after we sold it so we did benefit from the R.E.A. line there.

Our business expanded, unbelievably, during the years we were operating the resort on Napoleon Lake. We had friends who came to our resort regularly from Iowa, Illinois, Ohio and Indiana, in addition to our Minnesota patrons.

When we first ventured into the resort business, we were really operating on a shoestring, in a manner of speaking. On July 4 of our last year in business, our large yard was packed to the limit with cars and our driveway, which was a quarter of a mile long, was full of cars parked on both sides clear out to the end. So, you can see we did pretty well, despite our having been told by well-meaning folks there was no way we could make it in the resort business so far back in the boondoggles away from a main highway.

LOST TRACTOR

During our later years at the resort, I used to haul some timber around the country with a truck I had purchased. One day, I met a fellow on the street up at Bigfork.

"Edgar," he said to me, "would you consider hauling a load of corral posts out to Sheridan, Wyoming? My daughter lives out there. She has a dude ranch and she needs these posts to build a new corral."

"Sure," I said, "I'll take them out. When do you want to go?"

"Well, the sooner the better," he said. "Right away, if possible."

We proceeded to get his posts loaded onto my truck and then, of course, we stopped at the supper club to have a meal before we started. Now, they had a bar at this establishment and we got started imbibing. Consequently, I don't remember a whole lot about that trip to Wyoming!

I recall one stop we made en route: We bought a little red tractor that I thought I could put to good use in my logging operation. After purchasing the tractor, we proceeded driving on out to Sheridan. When we arrived at our destination, we unloaded the posts, got the truck turned around and headed back toward Minnesota.

One of the boys with me asked, "Edgar, what's the name of the town where we bought that tractor?"

"Oh, boy!" I said, "That's right, we did buy a tractor didn't we?"

"Yeah, of course we bought a tractor, but what town was it in?"

"What town was it in?" I responded. "Hell, I don't even remember what state it was in!"

We never did find that tractor. So, if you happen to see a little red tractor around the country that looks kind of lonesome, let me know about it. It could be mine!

Although I didn't realize it then, in all probability, I had been a confirmed alcoholic from the time I was a young lad. I just couldn't bring myself to face that reality about myself at the time, and our move to the resort hadn't helped matters any.

10

Hunter's paradise

When time and circumstances permitted, I did some trapping on the side, which provided us with extra income. In hunting season, I was kept busy serving as a paid guide for hunters who came up to shoot deer. Both Allie and I prided ourselves in being expert marksmen with a rifle, having done this sort of thing most of our lives.

One time when Marjorie was home for a visit she said, "Dad, can I take your rifle and go out into the woods?" She was about 13 or 14 years of age at the time, as I recall. We had taught her how to shoot a rifle, but had never permitted her to go hunting by herself.

"Sure, go ahead," I said. "Take my rifle and

go on out there and shoot yourself a deer." So she took my gun and left the house.

Allie and I both anticipated that she would probably walk into the woods several 100 yards and then decide to turn around and come back home. After she left, we got busy with some tasks that needed doing and more or less forgot about her for the time being. All of a sudden, "Ka-boom!" I heard a rifle shot from across the lake. Pretty soon, here came Marjorie with a great big grin on her face. She had shot and killed her first deer! Our daughter became an expert shot with a rifle during the ensuing years and was usually to be found on the firing line when hunting season rolled around each year.

DEER STAND

Along about this time, Bob Sharp (the fellow who helped get the Cadillac convertible out of the mud hole) and I came up with an idea for building a deer stand that hunters could sit on while hunting and then use to haul their deer out of the woods. This little contraption could be put to use in other ways as well, and we felt it showed some promise as a handy little invention.

Bob and I went down to Minneapolis and looked up some people we knew who did metal work of various sorts. They helped us bend some pipe for our project, which we brought back with us. Then, we went to Grand Rapids to a place where they fabricated plywood products. They used to buy birch and cut it into thin sheets for veneering, and fabricate it into various things.

We had some toboggans made to our specifications. Then, we fashioned some steps that could be attached to the toboggans. When all this was properly assembled, we came up with a deer stand that stood about six feet high. The idea was to lean this contraption against a tree, and use the toboggan for a seat upon which to sit while waiting for deer to come along. The entire device was securely strapped to the tree so it wouldn't fall over when the hunter's weight was on it.

When and if the hunter got a deer, the legs of the ladder were flipped over onto the toboggan and presto! You had the means with which to pull your deer to the desired destination. The strap was used to tie the carcass securely onto the toboggan. Every part of the device had its own purpose. No doubt about it, the thing worked pretty slick!

When we had the first model assembled, we took it down to Duluth. There was a fellow down there by the name of Rocky Teller who had a sporting program going and we thought it might be a good idea to show him our new invention. We decided to demonstrate the deer stand right there in his back yard, so we leaned the stand up against the clothesline and had Mrs. Teller crawl up onto the toboggan seat and sit on it. Unfortunately, we overlooked the matter of fastening the strap to secure it into its position firmly and Mrs. Teller wound up hanging by her neck in the clothesline. We got her out of the dilemma we had put her in as quickly as possible, before the poor woman choked to death!

Despite the unanticipated happening, Rocky could see that our deer stand had possibilities and that it was, indeed, a pretty good idea. So, we gave him one for himself and came back home. Soon after that, we went down to Minneapolis and had 100 of them built.

We talked it over and decided the first thing we had better do was to get a patent on our new invention. We were advised to mail a picture of the deer stand, along with a dated letter, to myself. Doing this would protect me from infringement on the idea until the patent came...so they said.

I got the idea of contacting a sporting goods company to see if we could make a deal with them to retail this item for us. We contacted one of the largest operators in the field of sporting goods in the entire country at that time. A goodly percentage of their yearly revenue was obtained through a big catalog that they published.

I had also heard that this company wasn't above jumping on someone else's patents if it got a chance to do so. I had no hard evidence that there was any truth to this implication, but thought it might be a good idea to tread a bit carefully in any dealings we might enter into with these people.

I came up with the bright idea of going directly to their own patent attorney and have him obtain our patent for us. That way, I reasoned, there would be less chance of getting bushwhacked than might otherwise be the case.

I was a little short of money at the time, so Marjorie, our daughter, loaned me the money to apply for the patent. The attorney's name was Dave and yes, he would apply for our patent for us. He informed us that it might take a year or more to receive the patent.

We waited and waited until a year and more had gone by without hearing anything from the patent office. Each time I made inquiry, Dave would inform me that he hadn't heard anything from them.

The next thing I knew, someone informed me they had seen an outfit like ours being exhibited at the big sport show down in Minneapolis. So, I went down there and sure enough, there was this guy demonstrating an exact replica of our deer stand!

"What is that thing?" I inquired of this fellow.

He said, "That's a deer stand."

I said, "It is?"

"Ya," he responded.

"Where did you get an idea like that?" I inquired further.

After he had given us a run-down on how he had acquired this product, I said, "Have you got it patented?"

"No," he replied. "I don't have it patented, yet; but I did make application for the patent about two weeks ago."

"Well now," I said, "I've got news for you. I applied for a patent on that deer stand more than a year ago."

"There's something a bit strange about all this," he retaliated. "We've got the biggest patent attorney in Minneapolis. Can't think of his name offhand, but the secretary in the office told us they had made a patent search in Washington D.C. and couldn't find any thing on it, anywhere."

By this time, it was obvious that something was badly amiss. I went back to Dave and confronted him about the matter of what was, beyond any doubt, our deer stand being displayed. I also informed him that a search had been made by the party now in possession of my invention and nothing was found indicating that any prior application for a patent on it had been made.

"Well," he then admitted, "I'll have to tell you the truth; I never applied for the patent."

I have always been a little on the hot-headed

side and when Dave informed me that he hadn't submitted the application for our patent on the deer stand, I was mightily tempted to get him by the throat and twist his head around about 180 degrees.

"Well, what do we do now?" I asked of him when I had gotten my temper somewhat under control. I didn't have the slightest idea what he would come up with in this matter and what he suggested came as somewhat of a surprise to me. He knew that if he didn't produce something that suited me pretty good, he was in for one helluva' lawsuit.

"Here's what we'll do," Dave said. "I'll get ahold of this other patent attorney and I will have a talk with him. I know him real well. I'll have him inform the man who now has your deer stand that they have made another search there in Washington, D.C. and found the original application." I decided right then and there that some of the things I had always heard about some attorneys, at least, were true.

Well, that's what he did. He informed the gentleman involved that another patent search had been made and the application found, etc. The man was also informed that he would have to buy the right to build it.

"What are we going to do about all this?" our competition asked after I had laid my cards on the table with him.

"It just so happens that I'm not in an overly favorable position to start marketing this product right away," I informed him. "So, if you folks want to buy it and go ahead and manufacture it, why, uh, I'll sell it to you."

That's what we did. I sold him the application for the patent and he went on ahead with it. I went out on the road and sold a big part of the 100 stands we had made. I gave the purchaser of our patent application the only one I had left. I've been sorry ever since that I didn't keep one for myself. I sometimes wonder how utterly stupid a person can be...and me, foremost of all!

HOT SHOTS AND ROOKIES

One year when we were getting things organized for deer hunting at our resort on Lake Napoleon, a hunter we had never seen showed up and made reservations with us. His name was Albert Nelson. He was a mail clerk on a passenger train that ran between Minneapolis and Chicago.

Albert was a quiet sort; didn't say a whole lot, but seemed to be a real nice fellow. The rest of my hunters were all out testing their rifles and getting ready for the big event. They had set up some targets to shoot and from where I stood observing them, they were hitting just about everything in sight except the targets.

Pretty soon, Albert picked up his rifle, an old Winchester lever-action, and sauntered out there to where the target practicing was taking place. "Ker-bang!" He hit the bull's-eye dead center. I decided right then and there that we had a man here who knew how to shoot a rifle.

The following day we went out into the woods. I had Albert positioned up in a tall jack pine tree while I was making a drive toward him. Unbeknownst to me, our dog had followed me out there. He had a white tip on his tail and from a distance, sort of resembled a deer running through the brush if you didn't look too closely.

Now, when I was makin' this drive in Albert's direction, this dog went around me and ran on up ahead. Then, "Ker-bang!" I heard Albert shoot. I heard that bullet ricocheting through the trees altogether too close to me for comfort. I had a notion to take a shot back at him to scare him a little, but thought better of the idea. What I was more concerned about than anything, was how my dog was making out. I was certain Albert had mistaken him for a deer, y'know.

I tramped on over to where Albert was stationed up in his tree and yelled up at him, "Albert, what did you see?"

"A couple of deer went flyin' by," he responded from his perch up overhead.

"Can you show me their tracks?" I inquired of him further.

Albert couldn't show me any deer tracks and I told him that he had nearly shot me and my dog when he had cut loose at what he thought was a deer. It scared the hell out of him and it had scared me, too, I'll tell you.

We hunted the rest of the day and I don't recall the rest of the hunters' having gotten anything when all of us arrived back at the house. We hunted four more days and on the fifth day, we decided to hunt in the forenoon and then everyone would leave for home. So we all hunted until noon and came back to the house.

Everybody was gettin' their things packed up to leave and paying their bills. I asked Allie if she would mind driving into town and getting a bottle of brandy so we could all have a drink or two before they took off. That was fine with her. She went in and brought back a bottle of brandy and we all sat around and had ourselves a few drinks. It wasn't long until we were commencing to feel a little foxy with that brandy circulating through our veins.

Now, Albert hadn't had good luck in bagging

a deer. He was still sort of shook up over having mistaken my dog for a deer a few days prior.

"Why don't we all go out and make one more drive for Albert?" someone suggested. It took some doing, but we finally got him talked into it. We took Albert out on Wolf Lake Road and got him stationed where I wanted him. Then, as the rest of us were making the drive, I heard Albert cut loose with his rifle. Bang! bang! bang! bang! bang! Five times I heard him shoot. When the rest of us came out to where Albert was, he had killed five deer!

Now, some of the others hadn't gotten their deer, so the extra ones Albert shot, in one fell swoop, filled their licenses. He had done a beautiful job of shootin' that day—just exactly what I thought he could and would do if he had the chance.

Albert never returned to our hunting camp after that. That deal with the dog had scared him to the point that he simply gave up deer hunting.

Another unusual episode happened real early on the first day of hunting season. All of the hunters had gotten their coats on, had gotten their guns out and checked over, and were getting ready to get into the car. Suddenly, "Kerbang!" Someone shot right outside the house. "My God," I thought, "did someone get himself killed here?" It was just breaking daylight and I couldn't really tell what was going on.

I looked all around and finally, a fellow by the name of Albin Duer came walking out of an outside toilet not far from the house. I figured his rifle had gone off accidentally.

"Albin, what in the world happened?" I asked him.

"Well," he said, "I was sittin' in there with the

door open and I saw this deer walk by, so I shot it."

I'll be darned if Albin didn't get a deer while he was sittin' in that outside toilet! Now, that ain't going to happen too often!

One of the problems I sometimes encountered was hunters getting lost out in the woods during our drives for deer. On one such occasion I had instructed the ones who would be doing the driving not to cross the road when they got to the people on the stands. This way, I would have a good idea where to find anyone who might have gotten separated from the rest of the drivers.

I had the hunters who would be doing the shooting that morning stationed at their stands awaiting the arrival of deer from the drive. Everything was working out according to plan, but one fellow didn't show up along with the rest of the gang of drivers. We waited for quite a while for him to show and finally decided that he had gotten himself lost out there in the woods somewhere.

I was just getting ready to go in looking for him when I heard somebody back the other way, west of us, start shootin'. The noise was coming from somewhere between us and South Fork Lake. Whoever it was, he was shootin', hollerin', screamin' and then he'd shoot some more. I knew from the way he was carrying on that something was radically wrong.

"Alvin, there's somebody lost out there," I said to one of the fellows. "I guess I'm going to have to go and see if I can find him. Now, you guys go in this way and I'll go the other way and we'll see if we can find our man. It sounds like he's over by South Fork Lake someplace."

So, I went down there and in about two miles or so, I found him. It was our man, all right. He had disregarded my instructions not to cross the road and not to walk more than 45 minutes in the event he hadn't come to the road by that time.

When I found him, he was yellin' and hollerin', and in a real state of emotional distress. The man was practically insane, scared half to death, had even thrown his gun and his jacket away. I finally succeeded in getting him calmed down a bit and escorted him out of the woods and back home.

The following morning he declined when the rest of us were getting ready to go out hunting. Not only did he refuse to go with us that morning, he never went back into the woods again. Getting himself lost the previous day had put the finishing touch on anymore hunting on his part. He'd had enough right then and there.

TOMMY DORSEY

One day I was walking down the road near a little old lake called Bass Lake. I met a man walking toward me on the road there and engaged him in conversation for quite a long time. As we visited, I kept getting the feeling that his face seemed familiar somehow, but I couldn't put a handle on it right off.

"Your name wouldn't happen to be Tommy, would it?" I inquired.

"It sure is," he replied.

"Tommy Dorsey?"

That's right," he responded.

"What in the devil are you doing way up here?" I exclaimed.

"Well," he said, "Harl Simmons, who lives

over at Zephyr Lodge, alongside the lake, is my uncle. I'm up here on vacation."

Now, Harl Simmons was the fellow I worked for in the sawmill for awhile. Harl was an executive with the Zinsmaster Bread Company. He also had a factory that made all the cutting and slicing blades for them. He was involved with a number of enterprises, into most everything. It goes without saying, how surprised I was in running into Tommy there.

I knew Harl Simmons quite well; he was a pretty good friend of mine, so I invited him to come over and hunt with us the next day. Sure enough, here came Harl and Tommy Dorsey and the rest of the gang and they hunted with us all day. So, that was a rather pleasant experience, getting the opportunity to meet a famous band leader unexpectedly.

MY DEER

When the deer season had about run its course, I decided I was going to take Marjorie, our daughter, out hunting. By this time, she was out of school and working in Minneapolis. She had been home with us at the resort for a short time, helping her mother with the heavy workload that always existed—cooking and what have you—during deer hunting season.

There were several deer hunters around yet, and we all decided to take Marjorie out there and make a drive for her. I had some of them line themselves up along Raddison Lake Creek and the rest of us were going to make the drive.

I knew where Marjorie was going to be, so I started up through the woods from a point about half a mile south of her, heading toward her. Pretty soon I heard a loud "Ka-bang!" and I knew she had gotten off a shot.

I kept coming toward her and pretty soon I came upon a deer lying beneath a balsam tree. It was crippled and trying to get up but couldn't and I knew that Marjorie had shot it. I proceeded to kill and gut it, then went on out. When I reached the point where she was she said, "Did you shoot my deer?"

"Whatta' you mean, shoot your deer?" I responded.

"My deer! Did you shoot my deer?" Marjorie demanded impatiently.

"Why no, I don't think I shot your deer. I did shoot a deer back there, ya."

Boy, did she go up in the air! She knew which way her deer had gone and she wasn't about to let me claim it and take the credit for shooting it, I can assure you! This was only one of the myriad times that Marjorie and I played tricks on one another for kicks.

You'll Get Used to It

One summer morning, I looked out and saw one of our customers from Iowa sittin' down on the dock all by herself. She was kind of a crabby bugger, but I decided to walk down there and chat with her awhile. As I was approaching her out on that dock, she called out to me, "Did you ever see a country where it can get so hot in the daytime and then turn so cold at night? And these mosquitoes! Sakes alive, they are something else! And that terrible cottage cheese that they sell at that Round Lake Store..."

Her negative attitude amused me and I started to laugh, which I don't think she appreciated very much. Knowing there wasn't too much chance of changing her attitude to any extent, I decided to tell her a little story of my own. Now, what this lady was really ticked off about was that she hadn't wanted to come up to our resort in the first place. She had wanted to go to the State Fair in Des Moines, but was out-voted by her peer group, who had opted for coming up here.

I said to my disconsolate guest, "You're just not used to strange places. I heard of a lady who went on a trip to New York City. She was walking down the street and finally came to the Empire State Building. She stood there, marveling at its tremendous height and began counting the stories from the bottom up; 104 stories. Then, she decided to do a recheck on this and started counting them from the top down. When she had concluded this count, she arrived at a figure of only 102 stories.

"Well, now, something's wrong here." So, she backed right out into the middle of the street and started to make yet a third count. About this time, a policeman came along and tapped her on the shoulder.

"By gosh, lady," he said, "it would hold a whole lot of hay, now, wouldn't it?"

That woman wasn't too happy over what she seemed to think my story was implying and I left her there in our hunter's paradise to commiserate all by herself.

The American Dream

11

Lives in transition

Keeping the road to our resort cleared of deep snow in the wintertime was a major problem. The snowplow would get to within about a quarter of a mile of our resort and then, Allie and I would have to shovel the snow off the road from where they stopped, on into our place. Snow blowers, snowmobiles and all the other contraptions we take for granted nowadays didn't exist way back then. If we could have had some of these more modern conveniences in those days, we would probably have stayed right there indefinitely. But for us, there was no alternative than to do what had to be done by hand.

BACK SURGERY

Allie's back was beginning to act up worse, what with the hard work she felt it was necessary for her to do. We kept going to various doctors who told us she had everything from arthritis to lumbago. They advised her to get more rest and gave her some exercises she should do on a daily basis. But, even with all this advice, her condition persisted and steadily grew worse.

Finally, we heard about a doctor from Rochester who was coming into Bovey, down south of us. He was highly recommended and we were advised to go have a talk with him, which we did. During our time with the good doctor, we thoroughly explained the history of her infirmity, from its beginnings with her fall at the skating rink quite a few years prior to that time.

"Well, folks," he said when we had finished filling him in on the situation, "the only way you're going to be able to get the sort of diagnosis you can depend upon, is to go to Rochester or the University of Minnesota. There isn't the proper equipment up in this country to accurately determine just what is wrong with her back."

"Doc, what do you think is the real problem here?" I asked.

"Frankly, I don't know. I would only be venturing a guess, were I to attempt to answer your question," he replied with admirable honesty.

"Can you recommend someone who can get to the bottom of all this?" I asked.

"Yes, I know of two doctors who are specialists in that field," he replied.

"Who are they and why hasn't someone told us about them before?" I questioned.

"Edgar, these people are not easy to get in to see," the doctor replied. "They are much sought after from far and near. It's pretty tough to get an appointment with them."

The doctor informed Allie and me that the names of the two specialists he had referred to were Dr. Peyton and Dr. French. Again, he reiterated how difficult it was to get an appointment with either of them.

"Could you try to contact them?" I pressed the issue. "Where are they located?" He then expressed his opinion that the only chance we would have to get in touch with either of the specialists he had named would be to go to the University, in person, and go through the proper channels to endeavor to make an appointment at some future date.

"Doctor," I persisted, "is their any good reason why we can't try to contact them by phone from here?"

"Well, yes, I guess we could give it a try," he responded somewhat reluctantly.

"I would certainly appreciate it if you would," I replied.

He put in the long distance call right while Allie and I were standing there in his office and it just so happened that Dr. Peyton was at the University Hospital at the time.

We listened as he explained to the person on the other end of the line what the symptoms of Allie's back problems were. When he had concluded his report, we could hear Dr. Peyton instructing our doctor to have Allie come down and he would take a look at the situation.

A few days later, we went down to the University Hospital and somewhat to our surprise, Allie was scheduled for her examination in short order. After checking her over thoroughly, we were instructed to come back in five or six days for Dr. Peyton's prognosis. "I'll see if I can have an answer for you at that time," was the way he put it.

"Edgar, this girl has a fractured vertebra in her back," Dr. Peyton informed me when we returned for his report on the findings of Allie's prior examination. "Now, I can operate on her and nine times out of 10, I can have her back on her feet in 10 days or so. In all fairness to you, however, I must inform you that there is about one chance out of 10 that the operation might paralyze her for life. I know this presents you with a difficult decision to face; however, it is my professional opinion that without the operation she will be paralyzed in three or four years."

The man was right, it was a sobering opinion that he had extended. It had been about 14 years that she'd been hurtin' and doctoring with her back and we hadn't been able to come up with the right answer during that time, seemingly.

"If I perform this operation," Dr. Peyton continued, "there will come a time, sometime in the future, when she will undoubtedly incur some arthritis in her back. I have shared with you, as honestly as I can, what the risks are in going ahead with the operation. What do you want to do?"

"Well, if you think that's what it is...," I replied.

"Excuse me, I don't *think* that's what it is. There is no doubt in my mind as to what the exact nature of the situation is. She has a fractured vertebra in her back," he said. It was an emphatic, authoritative verdict that commanded our respect. The decision to undergo the surgery was made right then and there.

The operation was scheduled and performed.

We were informed that it would be about 10 days before we would know exactly how successful it would prove to be. One day, near the expiration of the 10 days, I chanced to be in Allie's room at the hospital when Dr. Peyton came in to examine her. He jabbed a sharp pin of some sort into one of her toes and noted the response he had hoped would result. Then, he rendered an opinion that was music to our ears: "She's going to be fine," he announced with a smile and then, assuming his usual professional air, he turned and left us to ourselves.

NEW JOB

I stayed with our daughter, Marjorie, there in Minneapolis while Allie was recovering in the hospital. One day while at her place, I thought, "Why don't I go out and look for a job so I can have something to do while I'm sittin' around here?"

I went over to the Brinkton Corporation, a big company there, and inquired as to what my chances were of getting a job with them. Now, this was just a month or so before Christmas and they informed me that they were going to put on a few people at that time.

"You will probably be laid off at the end of the Christmas season," they told me, "but we can use you until then."

I signed on at Brinkton with every reason to believe it would be a job of only several weeks' duration. When Allie was able to travel, following her discharge from the hospital and a time of convalescence at our daughter's place, I took her back to our home in Grand Rapids, which we had purchased when we sold the resort. Then, I returned to Minneapolis and my work at the Brinkton Corporation.

Several days before Christmas, they called me into the office. I went there expecting to get my notice that I was being laid off. Well, there was a little surprise in store for me!

"Edgar, you have been doing a beautiful job," my boss opened the conversation. "Do you think you could handle the set-up work here at the factory?" For a moment, I was struck dumb.

"Mr. Tungsten," I managed to reply, "I haven't done any set-up work. I haven't even seen all of your machines." They had great big punch presses, tube-bending machines and other heavy equipment, the likes of which I had never seen in my life!

"Well," he said, "if our set-up man would stay with you for 30 days, could you handle this?"

"Yes," I responded, "if he'll do this, I think I can handle it."

Well, they raised my wages way up and put me on with this set-up man. The next day, I came in to go to work and my instructor got into an argument with the supervisor and quit. Oh, Man! Now I was in a pickle! There were 80 women and around 40 men working in that department and I had inherited the responsibility of setting up the machines for all of them!

In desperation, I got in touch with my supervisor and informed him that the only way I could see to handle this unanticipated development would be for me to come in four hours before the shift started and use that time to get the machines set up properly.

"Do you have any blueprints?" I inquired of him further.

"The fellow who just quit on us walked out of here will all of our blueprints in his head," he informed me. Beautiful, y'know! So, I commenced working four hours prior to and four hours following the end of the shift—sixteen hours at a crack.

I informed my supervisor that if he could get a man to help me, I might be able to get things going as they should be. So, they did get someone to help me and in short order, the whole project was progressing beautifully. In due time, I was solely in charge of the setting up of all those machines in the entire department. In record time, the production charts were hitting new highs, which I felt real good about.

MORTGAGE AVENUE

With things going as they were on my job at Brinkton, we decided to buy a house in Minneapolis and establish our residency there. We found what we were looking for in Brooklyn Center; a house that suited our needs, with a small down payment. It was located out on Morgan Avenue.

We discovered that most of our neighbors had purchased their homes with little or, in some instances, no down payment. So, some fellow across the street from us changed the name of the street to Mortgage Avenue. Some of the folks in the neighborhood weren't too happy with that, but that's what the street sign read for awhile, at least!

Marjorie, our daughter, helped us move our household belongings from Grand Rapids down to our newly-purchased home. We obtained a large, four-wheel trailer to accomplish the task and made three or four trips to get the items we felt we needed transferred to Minneapolis.

We got Allie moved into our new location, disposed of our home in Grand Rapids and wrapped up the loose ends incidental to the sale of our resort up on Napoleon Lake. When I returned to my job at Brinkton, it was a good feeling to have Allie and me living under one roof once again.

At this time, Marjorie was employed through Employers Overload. When local companies needed additional secretarial, bookkeeping or other office duties performed, they would contact Employers Overload and have them dispatch someone who was qualified to handle the particular job. Marjorie got her share and more of these calls, which spoke well for her proficiency in doing whatever the situation demanded.

Marjorie decided to move back with Allie and me after awhile. She continued working with Employers Overload for quite sometime, and later accepted a position offered her by the City of Brooklyn Center. Marjorie was the first female to work for the City of Brooklyn Center. She got the opportunity following a big shakeup in the way they operated the office. The office was located two or three miles from our place, which considerably cut down her commuting time to and from work.

All the while, things were going well for me at Brinkton. I had gotten a sizable increase in wages and we were really producing a good volume of business. Then, the Fourth of July rolled around and they decided to close down their operation for several weeks. Word was being circulated that some of the employees were to be laid off and although I didn't feel that I would be one of them, I did have some second thoughts about laying around for several weeks doing nothing.

So, I went to Charles Tungston, the president of Brinkton and asked him if he could give me a letter of recommendation so I could go to work for someone else until Brinkton started up again.

He said, "You don't have to go no place, Edgar. If you want to stay here, you can keep busy sweeping the floor, or whatever, and we'll pay you your wages..."

"No, I'd rather not do that," I interrupted. "I would rather go to work for someone else and earn my money."

Mr. Tungston wrote me a letter of recommendation and I soon found employment with Flower City Ornamental Iron Company on the far south side of Minneapolis. My daily trip to and from this new job took me past a large laundry firm that had a "Help Wanted" sign posted out front. When I mentioned this to Allie, who was recovering nicely from her back surgery, she decided to go down there and apply for work.

She got a job at the laundry, working the same shift I was working at Flower City Ornamental Iron Company, so I would drop her off at the laundry on my way to work and pick her up on my way home. This was about as convenient an arrangement as one could ask for.

PANCAKES AND SANDWICHES

Marjorie always got a kick out of playing tricks on her dad, and it would be fair to say that her dad derived an equal amount of pleasure in reciprocating. This particular incident took place on April Fool's Day. I'm not sure what year it was, but it was during the time that we were all living in the house at Brooklyn Center, while I was working for Flower City Ornamental Iron Company in Minneapolis.

"I'll cook some pancakes for breakfast this morning," I announced.

So, I went over to the stove and poured some pancake batter that I had mixed up into the skillet. Then, I fashioned a large pad of cotton and pressed it into the batter I had poured into the skillet. Finally, I added another layer of batter over the whole thing, making a "cotton-sandwich" pancake about 10 or 12 inches in diameter.

When this special pancake I had made for Marjorie was done, I took it over and placed it in front of her. She proceeded to put some butter and syrup on it and attempted to cut it into smaller sections with her table knife.

"Dad, this darned thing acts like it has cotton in it," Marjorie declared, when she had sawed away on it for awhile to no avail.

I couldn't help but burst out laughing and she knew right then and there she had been the object of an April Fool's joke, so she went over and tossed the whole mess into the garbage pail, accepting the prank like the good sport she always was. I figured that was the last that we would ever hear about the doctored-up pancake. But one April Fool's morning, quite awhile later, Marjorie informed her mother that she would fix my lunch pail. This wasn't anything unusual because they sometimes alternated in fixing my lunch pail.

When lunchtime rolled around down at Ornamental Iron, all of us workers filed into the room where we always ate our lunch and took our traditional places on the wooden benches provided for that purpose. I opened my dinner pail, poured a cup of hot coffee from my thermos jug, unwrapped the thick sandwich Marjorie had placed right on top and proceeded to take a big bite out of it. What happed next

170

was observed, firsthand, by several fellows sitting right next to me.

I pulled and pulled on that sandwich and suddenly a big beer label with mayonnaise all over it dropped down over my chin! It read, "Schmidt Beer," in large letters, I vividly recall.

Here, that little wart had stuffed all my sandwiches with beer labels and mayonnaise and the fellow sitting next to me, a guy by the name of Miller, witnessed the whole incident. He was laughin' up a storm and I'm sure watching me try to eat those sandwiches must have presented quite a spectacle! I don't know just how many people worked in that big factory, but the word spread like wildfire. Everybody in the whole plant knew about the trick that had been played on me, almost quicker that it takes to tell about it. These were just two of the many tricks Marjorie and I played on one another when occasion permitted.

BLUEPRINT FOR THE FUTURE

Ornamental Iron was a big company that specialized in building aluminum buildings of all kinds. Any fancy building, any kind of metal work that was called for, they could do it. They also had their own architectural department.

I had been working for this firm about 90 days when word came out that they planned to send nine men, out of about 1,000 employees, to blueprinting school. I'll be darned if I wasn't one of those picked out of that large group to go away to school!

The name of the school was Dunwoody Institute of Architectural Blueprinting. I had attended the institution for some time and was starting to get a pretty good feel of that profession when a quirk of circumstances tossed a monkey wrench into any future I might otherwise have had in the field of blueprinting.

Flower City Ornamental Iron Company had landed some big contracts, which included building the First National Bank in Minneapolis, adding a wing onto the White House in Washington, D.C., and some work on the LaGuardia Field in New York. For some reason, these contracts all went bad at the same time and had to be recalled and redone. I guess the bids were higher than what the clients were willing to spend.

Consequently, there was a big lay-off of employees at Ornamental Iron until they could get all this straightened out. Understandably, since I was younger in seniority than most, if not all, of those involved, I was laid off. Too, I hadn't had the opportunity to obtain the amount of practical experience in blueprinting to warrant keeping me in that program.

I went to work for Marquette Manufacturing Company and Allie was still working at the laundry. It was at this time that some things began to take place that would drastically change the course of our lives. Even now, nearly 40 years later, I sometimes have to pinch myself on the cheek to make sure if it really happened. It often seems as though it was only a dream that seemed real.

12

A business is born

It all started when I chanced upon nine deer feet we had brought with us when we moved to Minneapolis from Grand Rapids. While I was holding this package of deer feet in my hands, a mental image of a gun rack, complete with details of vivid clarity, sort of flashed into my mind out of nowhere.

It was to be a knock-down rack with two sides and two cross-bars mounted on a wood base. It could be a one-gun, a two-gun or three-gun capacity gun rack, which could be mounted on a wall in one's home or installed across the rear cab window of a pick-up truck.

Deer feet

Securing the deer feet to the wood base was the first problem that had to be worked out. So, I called Minnesota Mining and Manufacturing (3M) and explained to them what I wanted to do.

"Yes, we'll be glad to help you," I was informed when I had briefed the gentleman in their office as to what I had in mind. "If you want to come down..."

"It is a little difficult for me to come to your office," I said. "I'm working days at Marquette Manufacturing and I also work Saturdays."

"Well, can you come on Sunday?"

"Yes, you bet I can," I responded.

"We'll keep the place open for you," I was informed.

The following Sunday, I drove down to 3M and was admitted into the plant by guards stationed at the gate. I began to wonder just what kind of deal I was getting into. I was escorted to the office of the person I had been in contact with where I was cordially received.

He and his co-workers helped me all day long. Some plastic specialists helped me figure out a plastic grommet for the end of the deer feet, enabling me to secure them to the wood base by inserting the grommeted deer feet into a one and three-eights inch hole drilled in the wood.

After we had finished figuring all this out, this person informed me that if I would go to George Herter & Company, I could possibly buy the plastic material I needed for less than 3M could sell it to me.

I was finding it difficult to understand just why these folks at 3M were being so accommodating and I told them so.

"I appreciate the time you have spent with me," I ventured, "but I'm wondering why you would do this when you don't stand to profit from it."

"That's the way we learn. It is from outsiders that we get many of our new ideas," I was then informed.

So, I went down to Herter's and purchased the needed plastic and used my nine deer feet— eight, actually, since one of the original nine was used in our experimenting with the project—to assemble my first gun rack, which would hold four rifles.

At the first opportunity that presented itself to do so, I went to several large stores, including Corrie's Sporting Goods, Donaldsons Department Stores, Dayton's Department Store and Gokeys. After calling on these retail outlets, I had tentative orders for $1,800 worth of gun racks!

"Now, what are we going to do?" I asked Allie and Marjorie when I returned home with the fantastic news.

Marjorie, always the innovator, came up with the idea of writing to the state capitals to get lists of the locker plants in their respective states. Then, we would contact these locker plants to see if we could buy the needed deer feet from them. Now, this seemed like an excellent idea, but it would be time consuming and I was faced with the problem of filling these orders I had taken.

We managed to locate 90 deer feet up at

Effie, Minnesota, and were successful in finding quite a few more at several other places. I made up as many gun racks as my inventory of newly-acquired deer feet would permit, some of which were to be used as samples to show prospective buyers.

Then, we put up seven maps on the walls of one of our bedrooms and put red thumbtacks on them to indicate the locations of locker plants we hoped to deal with. We commenced writing these firms, telling them of our plans to start buying deer feet and that we would pay 10 cents apiece for them.

We learned a hard lesson in human nature in short order. At first, our stated price was satisfactory with our sources of deer feet, but as soon as they discovered they had a good thing going for them, they all started raising their prices, which soon became prohibitive.

We quickly learned to include a copy of our contract along with the letters of inquiry we sent to prospective locker plants. We also asked for an estimate of how many deer feet we could count on from them, based on the number they had during the prior year. This worked out quite well and we were constantly adding to our list.

No COLLATERAL

When our supply sources had been confirmed to our satisfaction, I packed up this data, along with the orders for deer feet I had taken, and went down to the bank to see if I could obtain a loan for the amount we had determined we would need to get this operation underway.

Before going to talk to the bankers, I thought it might not be a bad idea to avail myself with "an ace in the hole," as I was aware that my chances of getting the loan through regular channels might be pretty slim. Now, the man from whom we were buying our house in Brooklyn Center was an official of the Northern Pacific Railroad and I decided it might be a good idea to ask him to provide me with a letter of recommendation to take along with me to the bank.

Within short order, I got the desired communique from him. He informed me that he wasn't in the money-lending business, but suggested that I go to the Midland Bank to seek the loan and to take his letter along with me. I later learned that this official of the Northern Pacific Railroad, a Mr. Goodsell, as I recall, was a heavy stockholder at the Midland Bank.

When I went down to the bank, I was ushered into a private office of someone in the loan department. When I had stated my purpose for being there, he said, "How much do you need?"

"Well, about $5,000 to start," I replied.

"What do you have for collateral?" he inquired further of me.

"Well, all I have for collateral are these deer feet that I have on hand," I responded.

I could tell by the look on his face that I wasn't going to get very far in acquiring my $5,000 loan from him, with only my deer feet for collateral. This banker wasted few words in telling me that this sort of thing just wasn't done in his business.

"Oh, by the way, I have something here that I have been asked to present to you for your consideration," I rejoined, producing the letter of recommendation from Mr. Goodsell and handing it to him.

"Hmmm, hmmm," I could hear him murmuring to himself as he read the letter. When he had finished, he contacted the vice president of the bank on the intercom and asked him to come into his office. The vice president's name was Everett Swanson.

"Mr. Swanson," he said when the latter had made his arrival, "here's a gentleman who has a letter from Mr. Goodsell asking us to lend him a rather sizable amount of money. The conditions are somewhat irregular, but perhaps it might be a good idea to give the matter our careful consideration."

"Well," Swanson replied, "let's take a closer look at it."

Noting that the loan officer whom I had first approached about the loan had other loan applicants waiting to talk to him, Mr. Swanson had me follow him to his private office, where I was invited to take a seat while he read Mr. Goodsell's letter of recommendation. When he had finished, he turned to me and said, "What can we do for you?"

"Well," I said, "I'm going to have to buy these deer feet for the gun racks," and I showed him my contracts with the locker plants that we had lined up to provide us with deer feet in large quantities. I showed him the orders I had procured in the amount of $1,800. When I informed him that I had gotten these orders in only one day of soliciting the well-known firms I mentioned earlier, I sensed him developing at least a semblance of interest in my quest for a business loan.

He looked at the letter a second time and asked me how much I felt it would take to get the operation going. I informed him that I thought it would require at least $5,000. As the first person had done, Mr. Swanson inquired as to what collateral I had.

For the second time during that morning at

Midland Bank, I informed an official of that institution that all the collateral I had to put up was the deer feet in my possession. I was not unaware how utterly ridiculous such a premise for obtaining a large loan from a lending facility would have been had it not been for the fact that I had an influential stockholder of their bank backing me in my quest.

Mr. Swanson came out to our house to have a look at the place where we would be operating the gun rack enterprise. He seemed satisfied with several aspects of this arrangement, the potentially low overhead factor in particular.

We drove back to the bank and when we were back in his office once again, Mr. Swanson leaned back in his chair, clasped his hands behind his head and just looked at me in silence for a time. I wasn't sure whether to interpret the expression on his face as one of frustration or amusement. I didn't know what else to do, so I just looked right back at him awaiting his decision.

"Edgar," Swanson finally broke the silence, "this is one of the damndest transactions I've ever had to rule on. We've surely never been called upon to make a $5,000 loan to someone whose sole collateral adds up to some deer feet. The board is going to have reservations about my decision when I show them the deal. But you know something? I've got this gut feeling that you're going to pull this venture off. I'm going to grant you the loan."

Of course, I was overjoyed in all this, but there was just one stickler to the loan. It was for a period of 90 days. So, in the awareness that there was no way I could get everything into production and get the sales program set up efficiently in three months, I went to the Fidelity State Bank and sought an audience with a man there by the name of Herb Cornell, whom I had dealt with prior to that time. I presented him with a run-down of my plans to manufacture and sell the deer feet gun racks and showed him the draft from the Midland Bank.

"Where do we enter into the picture on this? he inquired.

"Due to the fact that I didn't have too much to offer Midland in the way of collateral, I had to settle for the 90 day stipulation in order to procure the loan. I did this, knowing full-well that it will not be possible for me to pay off this short-term note in that short a time.

"What I am proposing is this: I will pay off as much of the note as I can in the time limit that I have before it comes due and payable in full. At that time, I would like to have your bank pick up that note for me in order to keep my credit intact."

Herb Cordell turned in his swivel office chair and addressed his secretary who was doing some typing at her desk nearby, "Vi," he called over to her, "I don't know why and how we get into these kinds of messes, but we're going to help this guy with his problem."

So that was how I managed to get the financial arrangements made, enabling me to get started manufacturing those gun racks. When the unpaid balance of my note at the Midland Bank came due, the Fidelity State Bank picked up the note. When this came due, Midland reciprocated in the same manner; and so I dealt back and forth between those two banks until I got on my feet a little better and got rollin'.

BOOTIN' OUT GUN RACKS

Now that I had the operating capital to work

with, I went down to the lumberyard and bought a supply of walnut, oak and redwood, the three kinds of wood that the gun racks were to be made of. I got the racks all made up and that fall, the deer feet started rolling in. Boy, you can't believe how they were coming in!

About this time, we got an unexpected surprise that helped us out considerably with our finances. A man from Jon-E Hand Warmer Corporation came in and said, "Mr. Brooks, I understand you're going to be buying deer feet from all over the country."

"Yes, we are," I responded.

"Well," he continued, "y'know, I'm with Jon-E Hand Warmer and we would like to have the scent from those deer feet. We would like to put deer scent in our hand warmers."

I didn't even know deer feet had a scent and I was at a total loss as to why this fellow wanted to use this scent in their hand warmers. I pressed him for more information about all this.

"Here, I'll show you," he said and spreading the toes apart, he showed me where the scent gland was to be found. "That's the reason you always see a buck goin' along with his nose to the ground, sniffin'."

"We will send you a machine that you can use to go in there and extract scent from the deer feet," he continued, "and we'll pay you $36 an ounce for it." Well, believe me, that sounded pretty good to me; that was a big, big help for us.

I pickled the deer feet and did the rest of the necessary processing that was required in the basement of our house. My wood shop was out in the garage. Until I got my processing solutions prepared just right, those feet were creating somewhat of an undesirable odor in the basement. Marjorie was a bit discouraged with me for a time, but I finally got everything going along fine. In record time, we were making gun racks and shipping them all over.

The racks were knocked down and packed in a box. There were two boards for the sides and two cross-boards for the four-gun rack. There were eight deer feet on each rack and included in the carton were the printed instructions for assembling the components correctly. I don't recall exactly how many deer feet we used in our first year in business but during our final year in the taxidermy business, into which the gun rack business eventually evolved, we ran 40,000 of them.

When we saw what the potential of the business that I was now into really amounted to, Allie quit her job at the laundry and came home to help out. A little later, Marjorie quit her job at the Brooklyn Center City Office and joined forces with us, also. By this time, we were really bootin' out the gun racks!

One day, a fellow by the name of Russell Underdahl stopped by. He was quite a person to invest in out-of-the-ordinary enterprises. He wanted to enter into a deal with us to purchase large quantities of deer feet, which he planned to put up in nicely labeled packages and ship to various places; even as far away as Hawaii. He purchased about $2,500 worth of our deer feet before deciding it wasn't as profitable a venture for him as he had anticipated and dropped out of it. Needless to say, the $2,500 came in pretty handy along about then.

THE ALASKAN SHOP

As I recall some of the things that happened over the years, I get the feeling that unbeknown to us at the time, a Power greater than our own, was taking pretty darned good care of our best interests. Sort of charting the course for us, as it were.

In my rounds to the locker plants to pick up deer feet, some of the vendors began asking if we mounted deer heads and things like that.

"Well...I guess we could," I ventured.

"Well, by golly, would you take these deer heads with you?"

That was really the start of our getting into the taxidermy business. Soon, some birds commenced coming in and before long, we realized our house was too small to accommodate our growing business.

Along about that time, a man who worked for Corrie's Sporting Goods, down on Marquette Avenue in Minneapolis, came to me with an idea.

"Edgar," he said, "I've done some taxidermy work; how would you like to go into partnership with me in opening a taxidermy shop?"

The outcome of all this, in a nutshell, was that Bob Mishnick and I worked out a deal to go into business together. We rented a large store down on Hennepin Avenue and we timed our opening date to coincide with a big sport show scheduled to take place in Minneapolis.

Our booth at the sport show chanced to be right alongside the booth of a fellow from Alaska who was representing Johnson Outboard Motor Company. In the course of our conversation back and forth, we learned that he was a long-distance swimmer and quite the athlete. He had swum the English Channel and had also climbed the Matterhorn in Switzerland. He was currently practicing his swimming in Lake Mille

Lacs north of Minneapolis. His name was Harry Briggs.

My business partner and I got to wondering if the Alaskan products he was displaying in his booth might sell well in our soon-to-be-opened taxidermy shop. We approached Harry with the idea and he thought it might be worth a try. So, we added his line of merchandise to the other items in our store and opened it under the name "The Alaskan Shop."

In addition to the Alaskan products, we took on the Berman Buckskin line of jackets, moccasins and other miscellaneous buckskin items. Within a relatively short time, we began receiving some fish, deer heads and a growing assortment of birds to be mounted. In the early days of the business, hunters were bringing in pheasants and mallard ducks for the most part.

Things went fairly well in our new venture into the taxidermy business. Eventually, we worked out an arrangement whereby Allie and I went out on the road calling on prospective customers, leaving Bob Mishnick and his wife to run the shop during our absence. Allie and I traveled by auto to distant places such as Cincinnati, Indianapolis, Des Moines and Fort Dodge setting up taxidermy accounts with businesses that would ship their items to us for mounting.

In our travels around the Midwest, we were selling some gun racks and also getting rid of some ducks and pheasants. We made a favorable deal with a game farm to supply us with large quantities of pheasants to mount. The resale of these pheasants wasn't quite keeping up with the number of them we were taking in, despite the fact that several of our wholesale buyers had salesmen out on the road selling them along with their other lines of items. In the

final analysis, Allie and I were producing the greater portion of the pheasant sales.

I made a call from Indianapolis one day to check up on how things were going back home. My partner informed me that someone had contacted him wanting to sell these birds for us. Well, I thought perhaps this was just another fluke. Others who had tried hadn't done all that well.

"He would like to know how many birds he could get from us," Bob informed me. "Shall we give him a shot at it?"

"Well, we can try him out," I said. "Tell him he can have as many as he wants." Frankly, I harbored doubts about the outcome of the deal.

This fellow got on an airplane and flew to Dallas, Milwaukee, Chicago and I don't remember just where else. And, Boy! By the time we returned to Minneapolis from our trip out on the road, we were really in the bird business! This guy had proved himself to be a super salesman.

In the early days, our taxidermy business was predominantly wholesale in nature, with our orders coming from the accounts Allie and I had established while we were traveling on the road. As time went on, the taxidermy work coming in to us was evolving from smaller items to larger items, from birds and fish to moose heads and the heads of larger African animals.

One of the drawbacks of our location on Hennepin Avenue was our limited parking area. It just wasn't adequate to accommodate the expanding volume of customers who were now bringing their business in to us direct. It was becoming obvious that we would soon be needing a change in the location of our business that would provide us, not only a better customer parking facility, but adequate space to set up an assembly-line type of operation to expedite our overall operation.

Circumstances arose about this time that culminated in our buying out Bob Mishnick's equity in the business. So now, Allie, Marjorie and I found ourselves having to carry the whole load ourselves.

We scouted around and finally found a nice house out in Columbia Heights that suited our objective satisfactorily. When the word got out that we were planning to move our business from Hennepin Avenue to Columbia Heights, some well-meaning friends began to admonish us that we were making a big mistake. Paradoxically, this advice was coming from the same sources who had sternly warned us that we couldn't make it down on Hennepin Avenue at the time we moved our business from Brooklyn Center.

"It just won't work out," they had told us at that time. "There's no way a taxidermy shop can be a successful undertaking if it is located on one of the main streets of Minneapolis. No way!" Their thinking wasn't entirely without some basis, for out of six new businesses that started on Hennepin Avenue at the same time we did, ours was the only one that survived. The rest failed.

If there have been any absolutes in Allie's and my somewhat adventurous life, they have consisted of the negative reactions on the part of well-meaning friends each time we ventured into some new project.

At the time we left the farm and moved to Napoleon Lake, we were told we were making a big mistake. "There is no way you can open up a summer resort so far back in the boondoggles, away from a main highway," we were advised. When we declared our intentions of opening our first taxidermy shop in Brooklyn Center, we were informed in no uncertain words, "It won't work. You're doing something foolish." And once again, true to form, we were getting the yellow-flag warning signals from close friends. Had we heeded the advice of these "do-gooders" along the line, Allie and I would never have left the farm. We would, in all probability, still be out there in the boondoggles, a few miles north of Buck Lake, milking cows and slopping hogs.

MONTANA HUNT

Before we moved in, Allie and I had drawn up the plans for some needed changes in the newly-acquired house in Columbia Heights. We decided that while the remodeling was being done, it would be a good time for the two of us to go on a hunting trip.

Over the years, we had been putting up a large display booth at the annual sport show in Minneapolis. During one of the shows, we had met a fellow by the name of Merlin Hartkopf, who owned a hunting camp out in Montana. Merlin invited us to come out to his facility to hunt moose, deer or elk when the season opened. We had to draw for moose permits and were aware of the fact that only two permits would be issued in Minneapolis. Allie has always been lucky in any kind of drawing and sure enough, she drew one of the two for the Montana hunting trip. One other time, she drew for a similar permit for a hunting trip in north-western Minnesota and got one of those. If you want any drawing done for a lucky ticket of some kind, let Allie do it for you! She was even lucky enough to draw me!

We made our reservations for the trip out to Merlin Hartkopf's camp but for some reason, a mix-up occurred and when we arrived at his mountain camp, it was full-up. No vacancies. We went to Ennis, Montana, to make inquiries as to where we might find another hunting camp. While there, we chanced to run into Merlin Hartkopf and informed him that we couldn't get a place to stay out at his camp. He invited us to come stay the night at his house until he could make the necessary arrange-ments to get us into the spot we had reserved. We spent the night at Merlin's house and moved into his hunting camp the following morning.

We weren't too long in discovering several aspects to the operation we hadn't anticipated. In the absence of modern, indoor toilet facilities, we assumed they were using outdoor privies, instead. We were in for quite a surprise the first time nature called!

Instead of an outhouse, the toilet facility con-sisted of a sturdy pole, nailed laterally between two trees. You had to perch yourself up on that cross-pole and be damned careful you didn't fall off it! That could be embarrassing! Well, like it or not, that was the situation we had to cope with while there. Using that "bathroom" was quite an experience, I'll tell you!

The next thing we discovered was that Merlin didn't get his hunting parties underway as early in the morning as we had anticipated. We would get up early and have our horses all saddled up and ready to go, but it would invariably be 9 a.m. or later by the time we got out into the hunting area. Now, elk and moose are done moving by that time. Then, along about 3 p.m., we would all return to camp.

After several days of this, Allie and I decided to strike out on our own. We hadn't done well in spotting any moose, let alone getting a shot off at one. So, we took to getting saddled up and taking off up into the mountains real early, all by ourselves.

This one particular morning, we were topping a little rise when I thought I saw an elk back in the brush. But when it broke out into the open, it turned out to be a huge bull moose. I didn't have a moose permit of my own, so I said to Allie, "Here comes your moose."

This ol' boy came on down in front of us, his nose to the ground. He was snuffin' and puffin' and uttering a funny noise as he moved along.

Allie shot five times and that moose never broke stride, just kept walkin' along as if nothing was happening. When he finally dropped, after her fifth shot, we walked down there. She had hit him all five times and you could cover all five holes with one hand! They were all right on his front shoulder, exactly where they were supposed to be.

I'll have to say right here and now, that when it comes to shootin' a rifle, Allie is about as good as they come. I've seen her shoot deer, antelope, moose and what have you, and I've never seen her miss. Our daughter, Marjorie, also became a crack shot with rifle and shotgun.

After shooting the bull moose, we went back

to camp to get some help in hauling it out of the woods. Merlin was in town at the time and was gone all day, so we couldn't go out to bring the moose in until the next morning. We had brought a freezer along with us from Minnesota and we put the dressed meat in it after we got the moose hauled back to camp.

Allie and I got up early again the next morning to go deer hunting. I shot a deer, which we brought back to camp with us. Mrs. Hartkopf was planning to drive to Ennis in her van that day and said she would be glad to take our deer in with her. Ennis was about 50 miles from camp, so we thought that sounded like a good idea.

Somehow, during the trip to Ennis, Mrs. Hartkopf spilled a can of gasoline on the deer meat, which spoiled it for eating. We also had bad luck with the meat off the moose Allie shot. I've never seen meat do what this did. It would be nice and red when you first cut steaks from it and it wouldn't be fifteen minutes until the steaks would turn green. We had to throw all of it out and the bears wouldn't even eat it!

The Minneapolis paper carried a nice story along with a picture of Allie and her moose, which proved to be close to a record specimen. We mounted the head and it turned out beautiful. Sometime after we had quit the taxidermy business, a fellow from Peterson's Hardware in Coleraine came to our place and wanted to buy it. So Allie sold him her moose head.

Merlin Hartkopf's hunting camp was just behind Quake Lake, not too far from Yellowstone National Park on the Madison River. Quake Lake formed after a big earthquake shook the entire area. There were huge landslides coming down from facing slopes of two mountains into an area where a campground

S. Lowell Roberts

had been located. The landslides covered a large number of automobiles and most of them are still buried beneath all that debris.

I had a friend named Gaylord Gates who was parked in that campground just days before the landslide. He had been parked there for three or four days when he and his wife decided to move to some other location. It was a good thing they did, as it turned out.

When Allie and I were doing our hunting out there, we would go right up over that crater and on back to where we wanted to hunt. Let me tell you, this is the most beautiful country you can imagine—beautiful, beautiful country.

We saw a lot of sheep on the high peaks in the surrounding area. Lots of moose in there, too. From the tops of the mountains, we could see a deep fault that went right through the whole area. Land that went right along the side of the mountain before the quake had dropped about 12 inches or so, and now that fault stretches all the way along there. It was really impressive and I wondered where in hell all that ground could have gone.

The mountain horses we rode while hunting were something else. When we got ready to return to camp at night, we would come out on top of one of those cliffs above a huge rock slide. The rocks stretched far down to a creek at the bottom that looked smaller than it really was from our perspective. At first, we wondered how in the world we were supposed to get down to where we wanted to go.

The guide had told us, "Just aim your horse down that hill and sit still; that's all you have to do. He'll go right on down there." And he did. The sparks would be flying' off those horses' metal shoes all the way down those rocky slopes and believe me, it was a pretty scary ordeal! Those horses were really sure-footed.

It was a trip that Allie and I enjoyed immensely. Fortunately, both of us had been used to roughing it all of our lives, so the lack of modern conveniences at the Hartkopf hunting camp wasn't as difficult for us to cope with as it might have been under different circumstances.

The trip back to Minneapolis provided Allie and me ample time to reminisce on the past and the incredible amount of good fortune we had been graced with since we were first married. So many things had fallen into place in just the right time and order. We reflected on our progression from being "hicks from the sticks" to people who were now commencing to "rub elbows" with persons who really were somebody. Such a transition was truly remarkable, we concluded. It's not often someone whose formal education ended with the eighth grade and whose life has been lived for the most part in backwoods country realizes the achievements I have been blessed to experience. Allie did go to high school for one year, which served us well in our attaining the degree of success we were experiencing.

Now, lest it appear otherwise, in no way am I trying to take all the credit for our eventual success in the taxidermy business. Allie and Marjorie deserve as much or more credit than me. Minneapolis newspapers were a great help to us in promoting our business. The television stations put us on the air time after time after time. Banks cooperated with us when we needed their services. And I would be remiss if I didn't attest to the fabulous manner in which officials in the City of Minneapolis helped us get our business started.

13

Satisfaction guaranteed

When we arrived back at Columbia Heights, the major portion of the remodeling had been accomplished. Basically, all that remained was the task of putting up the large sign an advertising firm had built to our specifications, and that was soon accomplished. Confronting us, now, was the challenging project of moving our equipment and inventory from downtown Minneapolis to our new location and disposing of our shop on Hennepin Avenue.

In the new operation, we had worked out a plan whereby Marjorie would do the bookkeeping, I would do the general taxidermy work and Allie would take care of the more artistic aspects of finishing off the bird bodies and the bodies of smaller animals, plus painting the fish. This proved to be an efficient division of labor and soon after our grand opening, business began coming in like a huge tidal wave...and it never stopped.

Prior to our moving from Hennepin Avenue to Columbia Heights, a large percentage of our taxidermy work had been comprised of mounting birds and fish on a sublet basis for a number of sporting goods stores to whom hunters and fishermen had brought their trophies for processing.

Within an incredibly short period of time after getting settled into our new location, taxidermy business began coming to us direct in ever-escalating volume. It soon became necessary for us to discontinue taking in outside work from our former sources of supply.

Along with our expanding patronage from sportsmen who wanted their more highly prized items mounted, there was a growing demand for our duck and pheasant head wall plaques. Montgomery Ward, with some 8,000 stores scattered throughout the United States, became one of our foremost outlets for these popular items.

The Florsheim Shoe Company placed an order with us for 5,000 pheasants. They wanted one for each of their stores located all around the country. Hart Schaffner & Marx Clothing Company sent us an order for 5,000 birds at one time.

Trying to keep abreast in filling these large orders necessitated our expanding our work force from Allie, Marjorie and myself to nine employees in our Columbia Heights operation. A little later on, we opened a shop in South Dakota to take some of the load off of the Minneapolis enterprise.

In due time, we were shipping our head

plaques and birds, along with other items made in our shop, not only to most of the major outlets in the United States, but pretty much all over the world. Abercrombie and Fitch, Marshall Field's, and Neiman Marcus down in Texas, were to be numbered among our regular customers. Even the Merchandise Mart in Chicago started handling our products, which was a tremendous outlet in and by itself. Needless to say, all of this was becoming a challenging and increasingly stressful embroilment.

In case you may be wondering where we were getting all of the birds needed to make these thousands of wall plaques, we had contracted with large game farms, who were now raising birds exclusively for us. We had Wild Wings of Oneka in Hugo, Minnesota, raising them. The *Minneapolis Star and Tribune* had a large game farm that was supplying us with birds. Fred Armstrong from Anoka, along with several others, were selling us pheasants and ducks in goodly numbers.

PRICE OF SUCCESS

Whereas it was true that we were experiencing a keen sense of fulfillment in the incredible degree of success that was thrusting itself upon us, we were becoming increasingly aware that success at times has a high price attached to it. In our case, that price tag was in the form of stress that we were undergoing day after day, deriving itself from the torturous pace we were struggling to maintain without any let-up.

Not helping matters in all of this was the fact that I was still "experimenting" with that doggone liquor. It didn't take long for me to realize that this taxidermy shop was presenting me with even more occasions and excuses to drink booze than the summer resort up on Napoleon Lake had provided and, Lord knows, that was ample. Now, liquor was commencing to come in from all over the world!

If I could stay on my feet, I could still do a pretty good job with the taxidermy, but I couldn't always stay on my feet! Now, when I couldn't stay on my feet, I would cross the street from our shop to a filling station that did welding. I would go over to the acetylene tank and turn on the oxygen, taking a number of deep breaths of pure oxygen. Most of the time, this would help put me back in business, but sometimes not.

When the "oxygen therapy" failed to work, I would go on down the street another block or so to a doctor's office that was located there. The good doctor would give me a shot in the arm at my request.

Now, I don't have the slightest idea as to what was in that stuff he was shootin' into me, but I think it might have been the same formula they use to tranquilize bears. Soon after it got into your bloodstream, you were gonna' go to sleep, boy!

As soon as I had gotten my shot, I would tear out for home just as fast as my legs could get me there—down the street, across the sidewalk, through our yard and into the house. Once inside the house, I would zip through the living room and on into the bedroom and I'd stand there shiverin' and shakin' until the bed went by just right in my dizzy state. Then I'd dive into it, clothes and all, and there I would be for the next two or three days!

My wife and daughter would be out in the other room making excuses for me as to where I was at the time. I was either out-of-town or wherever they could think up a place for me to be. Anyplace but where I was supposed to be.

Those were difficult times for all of us, to be sure. I owe a tremendous debt of gratitude to my wife and daughter, without whose patience and understanding things would have turned out a lot different than they did. They were a tremendous help to me.

GET IT RIGHT

We now found ourselves dealing with people

from all over the world. Our patronage was consisting of such names as President Lyndon Johnson, President Richard Nixon (Presidents L.B.J. and Nixon didn't bring their business to us in person, but had it sent to us) and John Connally, then Governor of Texas. Other customers we had included Bing Crosby; JoAnne Castle, who used to play slapstick piano for Lawrence Welk; Ernest Tubbs, the guitar player and his band member, Leon, just to name a few.

Speaking of John Connally, I'll never forget the day President John F. Kennedy was assassinated in Dallas, back in November of 1963. I was carrying a large fish that had been caught up in the Arctic to the location in the basement where the fish were processed for mounting. Suddenly, over the radio, came the flash announcement that President Kennedy had been fatally shot. Then, followed the announcement that Governor John Connally had also been wounded. I nearly dropped that fish, for it was John Connally's fish I was carrying!

He had gone up to Chantry Inlet, on the Arctic Ocean, with a flying service from International Falls that I was familiar with. He had caught his big fish up there and had sent it to us for mounting. A coincidence such as this defies credulity. The odds against this kind of thing were astronomical by anyone's calculations.

On one of the days that the Oswald shooting was shown on television, I had placed my 16mm movie camera, mounted on a tripod, in front of the set and focused on the screen. I also got good pictures of that event. I got pretty good pictures of President Kennedy's funeral by following that same procedure. The best part of those pictures was that beautiful black horse prancing gallantly, with empty saddle, behind the horse-drawn caisson in the funeral procession. That portrayal on television was one that struck millions of saddened people with intense emotional impact, and Edgar Brooks was no exception. Tears flowed that day at Brooks Taxidermy Shop in Minneapolis.

Allie, by nature, has always been a very meticulous person. This quality in her makeup served our business in good stead because we were now finding ourselves doing work for people who didn't care how much they paid to have their items processed, so long as the work was done to perfection.

We took Allie to the Arctic Ocean numerous times and to many different places to observe firsthand the intricate colorings of various varieties of fish. One of the species we encountered a problem with was the Arctic grayling caught up around the Fifty-second Parallel. Grayling in that area area are somewhat copper colored, with a bluish strip on the back fin. Allie was painting all the grayling those colors, reproducing the hues as perfectly as it could possibly be done.

We had contacted Jim Peterson, who was writing a sports column for the *Minneapolis Star & Tribune* at that time, and Les Kouba, the artist who painted the federal duck stamp three times or more, to have them do some research on fish colors for us. They were going to make a trip up to Reindeer Lake, so we asked them to take some pictures for us. The pictures they brought back to us confirmed the authenticity of our coloring on the grayling.

It wasn't too long after this that we began getting criticism from some of our customers to the affect that we weren't getting the colors just right.

"Where are you fishing?" we asked them.

199

36-POUND NORTHERN CAUGHT IN CANADA

They informed us that they "were going north," and that's about all we had to go by. So we loaded Allie on an airplane and took her up to Reindeer and then on up to Great Bear Lake.

It was then we learned that the farther north you go, the darker in color the grayling get; and when you reach the Arctic Ocean, they become nearly iridescent. When turned over in the light, they'll turn from real dark to a purplish color. Different hues were produced depending on how much the light was striking their scales. The bluish strip around the back fin was constant, as was a little black spot under the chin.

Almost all species of fish have an identity all their own. Smallmouth bass have a white comma on the gill plate and walleyed pike have a white tip on the tail and white coloring on the lower back fin. The back three sections of the dorsal fin are always black.

Fishermen become familiar with the individual markings that the fish they specialize in carry. As a taxidermist, you have to know just what these markings are in each case, or you

find yourself in deep trouble. We felt it was necessary to make personal trips whenever possible
in order to become knowledgeable of the intricate details involved in turning out a finished
product that was as near perfect as it could possibly be. Our good reputation covered a vast
area of the United States as well as foreign
countries, and I am convinced that it was our
willingness to "walk that second mile" to satisfy
our customers that accounted for this success.

When we started getting more and more wild
animals that had been shot in Africa or Asia, figuring out a way to get them done up just right
posed an even greater problem than the Arctic
fish had presented. We couldn't afford to make
trips to those far-away countries to determine
exactly how they looked, so we started making
trips to zoos in various parts of the United
States to accomplish this end. We used the St.
Louis Zoo a lot because it was one of the best in
the country.

One fellow, for whom I had done a lot of
work, brought a wildebeest into the shop to
have it mounted. I did the job the way I thought
it should be, but when he came in to get it he
said, "Oh, Edgar, that nose is way too wide." The
man's name was Mel Hetland.

I said, "Mel, I think it's just perfect."

"No way," Mel responded.

So, I drove down to St. Louis with my camera
and took some pictures of a wildebeest's nose
and brought them back and showed them to
him.

"Well, Edgar," Mel said, when he had exam-
ined them closely, "I guess I'll have to concede
that you were right and I was wrong."

Yet another example of how some of these big-time hunters and fishermen operate is one that actually took place some years later, but it fits in nicely with the sort of unusual episodes that cropped up now and then during the years we were in the taxidermy business.

It had gotten to be commonplace for items of every description to be flown in to the Minneapolis International Airport, mostly from the Arctic. Sometimes this stuff would arrive around midnight, sometimes later than that. Then, Allie and I would have to go down to the airport to take these fish off the plane from people who were going on through to Ohio, Illinois or Lord knows wherever. Sometimes, there would be as many as 75 items that had to be sorted and tagged when we got back home. Many times, Allie and I worked nearly all night until the wee hours of the following morning doing this. We had four or five deep-freezers that we stored them in until we could get at them. It was getting to be a regular mill race trying to keep up with the business that was now coming in to us in ever-increasing volume. One day, we got a bunch of fish in that was tagged from a man living in England.

Well, we got those fish mounted up as quickly as possible and several days after we completed the project, we got a long distance telephone call.

"Hello!" came a cheerful voice over the line. "This is John Appleby from jolly ol' England. I was wondering how the fish I shipped to you from the Arctic are coming along. I assume you got them all right."

"Yes, Mr. Appleby," I replied. "We got them

61-POUND LAKE TROUT

O.K. We have finished mounting them and I've written you for a deposit."

"Mr. Brooks," my caller responded, "I have world banking facilities. A Minneapolis bank will pay you. How much is it?"

I told him how much the bill came to and he informed me what bank would pay us the money. He hung up without further adieu. About 30 minutes later, the phone rang again.

"Hello, this is John Appleby, again. I was wondering if it would be all right if my brother and I flew over to Minneapolis to have a look at my fish, firsthand. I've been having fish mounted all over the world. I've had some jobs done for me that I wasn't too happy with."

"Why sure," I said, "If you come over here you can see them."

"Fine," he replied. "My brother and I will fly over there on New Year's Day."

About 30 minutes later, the phone rang

again, and by now a familiar voice came over the long distance line for the third time.

"This is Appleby, again, from jolly ol' England. What's the fastest way to find you from the Minneapolis Airport?"

I said, "You just tell the Yellow Cab driver at the airport that you would like to go to Brooks Taxidermy. They haul fish out here all the time and they will know exactly where to bring you." And he hung up again as abruptly as before.

So on New Year's Day, John Appleby and his brother flew in and we showed them the fish. John shared several stories with us while here. He was a rather comical fellow who I judged to be about 45 years of age. It was divulged that this new customer of ours was an exceedingly wealthy person who manufactured all of the instruments for the Royal Air Force in England.

Before leaving to return home, John left detailed instructions as to how he wanted his fish shipped. Rather than having them flown by air freight, he stipulated that we were to arrange for them to be shipped in the passenger section of the plane and shipped to him C.O.D. In other words, we were to have them placed in the passenger seats, which would cost him the same as a first class ticket for human passengers. This was a new one for us, that's for sure!

"Just send them to John Appleby, C.O.D.," he repeated, noting my obvious amazement over his shipping instructions. "They all know me; they'll know who I am. When you're ready to ship them, just call the airport and they will send somebody out to pick them up."

So that's how his fish got from Minneapolis to England—not in shipping crates stacked in the freight section of the plane, but carefully placed, individually, in the passenger seats! It cost him several hundred dollars to fly those fish home.

Now, there is another paradox to this story. Some time later, we got a long distance call from John Appleby's private secretary.

"Mr. Brooks," he said, a note of anxiety manifesting itself in his voice, "we've had a terrible accident over here."

"What in the world has happened?" I inquired.

"Our janitor broke a fin off of John Appleby's favorite fish that you mounted for him. John is all shook up about the accident and wants to send it back to you to be repaired."

"That shouldn't be necessary," I informed the caller. I then furnished him with the name of a firm in London, one of the largest in the world, whom I felt sure could do the job.

"Nope," Mr. Appleby's secretary responded quickly, "he's going to send it back to you. He wants you to do the repair job for him."

Within a short time, the damaged fish arrived, first class as before. Once again, it cost him whatever a round-trip ticket would cost for a human passenger!

We had occasion to do lots of business for John Appleby (from jolly ol' England) during the ensuing years, even after we had eventually closed out our business in Minneapolis and moved back to Buck Lake. We have had occasion to ship him as many as seven mounted fish at one time, which resulted in his having to pay for seven reserved seats at one time. Money meant nothing, whatsoever, to this gentleman.

It so happened that John had shipped us seven fish to be mounted, which we hadn't completed before moving time rolled around, so we brought them with us to finish after we got set up in our new place back at Buck Lake. In fact, we were nearly eight years getting backlogged work of this nature completed after our move to Buck Lake. These items were kept preserved in deep-freezers until we could get at them. We still marvel that so many of our old customers were willing to wait so long for us to mount their items when they could have taken them to someone else.

When we did get John Appleby's seven fish processed, I took them over to Hibbing, intending to follow former procedures in having his fish shipped by air, first class. I met with their flat refusal when I informed them that they were to be shipped on first class seats normally reserved for fare-paying passengers.

"No way will anybody do this. That's impossible." I was told.

I should very definitely have hauled John's fish down to Minneapolis and put them on a plane there, but I didn't. Instead, I went to the local Railway Express and asked them if they could get the shipment loaded on seats in the passenger section of an overseas flight.

They informed me that they might not find it possible to have them loaded on the reserved seats as had been done on prior occasions, but they assured me they would get these fish on the plane. So, I turned them over to the Railway Express and to the best of my knowledge, they got them on the plane. In any event, that's the last we ever heard from John Appleby.

14

People business

As time went on, our business continued to grow by leaps and bounds. It became necessary for us to enlarge our work force, which eventually reached nine in number. Still, we could never quite keep up with the escalating volume of new business.

The upstairs living quarters of our place in Columbia Heights was commencing to look more like the storage section of a warehouse than a private home. Deep freezers, in which incoming objects to be mounted were kept until we could get to them, were now to be found in the bedrooms, the living room and even spilling over into the parlor.

We purchased a second house over in St.

Anthony to serve as our living quarters. It wasn't long until the same thing was happening there. Backlogged business was being stored wherever we could find space to put a freezer to keep the unprocessed birds and fish, and we were stacking the inventory of packaged items manufactured for wholesale and retail distribution in every nook and cranny about the place.

One thing can be said about all this. We were never bored! We never knew from one minute to the next what new direction any given operation we might currently be engaged in would suddenly assume.

DUCK BLIND

One day when I was in the office on the first floor of our place in Columbia Heights, the telephone rang. I picked up the phone and chancing to glance out the window at the same time, noticed a fellow standing in a public phone booth located almost directly across the street from our place.

"Brooks?" came the voice over the line. "Is this the Brooks that does the taxidermy work?"

"Ya, that's me," I said.

"Where in the world are you people located?" he stormed. "I've been all over this town and have struck out every time. Can you direct me to your place?"

"Where are you now?" I inquired.

"I'm at Thirty-seventh and Central."

I knew, then, that the guy I could see in the telephone booth was the one who was talking to me. I informed him that if he would turn around and look across the street from the phone booth, he would find the answer to his question.

"Oh boy!" he responded, "I can't believe this! I'll be right over."

When he entered the shop he started making all kinds of excuses as to why he didn't happen to see our place of business. We were getting his business taken care of when another gentleman came walking into the shop. Walking right up to me he said, "Mr. Brooks, I have a very unusual request to make of you."

"You do?" I replied, wondering what might be coming next.

"Yup," he said, "I would like to have you make a duck blind for me."

"A duck blind," I countered, a bit confused at such an unusual request.

"What I'd like to do," the newcomer continued, "is to get a steer hide and have you tan it for me. Then, I would like a zipper installed in it and the head mounted on the steer in its natural position, but in a manner that will allow it to move up and down.

"Now, when you have finished your part, I want to take it to a cabinet shop and have the whole carcass ribbed up so it has the appearance of a live animal. Then, I'll take all this to a company that manufactures electric scooters and have the carcass mounted on a scooter.

"I want to have the head move up and down so it looks like the animal is eating grass. I'll have a little glass windshield placed in the head to look out through while we're riding inside this contraption right down to a spot where ducks or geese hang out. When the time is right, all we'll have to do is unzip the big zipper, extending horizontally across one side, to create the opening for us to shoot out of.

"This guy has to be nuts," I thought to myself.

"What would having you make this for me cost, approximately?"

I hadn't had ample time to give the matter much thought so I said, "$400 should do it."

"Oh, that's not bad; not bad at all," he responded. "Where in the world could I get ahold of a steer hide? Where can I buy a steer?"

"I don't think you will need to buy a steer," I replied. "We can call the Johnsville Locker Plant and have them sell you a steer hide."

So, I called out there and explained to them what this guy wanted to do.

"You send this fellow out here," the man said, "and we'll sell him any steer hide he wants."

The man went out to Johnsville Locker Plant and when he came back, he had a big white-faced steer hide. As it turned out, he did buy a steer instead of just a hide and had all the meat out of it, too. He was from Watertown, South Dakota, and he was going to take this meat home with him.

We went ahead and constructed this unorthodox duck blind exactly to the specifications we had been given. Somehow, WCCO Television heard about it and asked us if there was any way we could set the whole thing up out in the yard so they could get some pictures of it.

Well, we put an air mattress in the back and our daughter and another kid we had working for us got it out into the front yard. Then, they got inside the steer carcass with shotguns and went through the motions of shooting game birds out through the zipper opening on one side of the portable blind.

Pretty soon, everyone who chanced to be driving down that street was stopping to see what Dale Hirt and Marjorie, inside the steer's midsection, were aiming at. There was an intersection up the street a short distance and before long, traffic was backed up for two or three blocks in all directions! The cops came out and had quite a time getting the traffic unsnarled.

The people from WCCO Television came out and got pictures not only of the uniquely constructed goose and duck blind, but of the traffic jam as well. An article appeared in the newspaper about all this, too. I still have the pictures and the newspaper article in our large scrapbook.

FUMBLING THE BALL

Shortly after the duck blind episode took place, a man walked into our shop one day who had recently returned from a hunting trip up in Canada with Rusty Meyers Flying Service. As usual, I was up to my armpits in whatever project I was working on at the moment and I didn't really pay all that much attention to him when he came in. People were constantly coming and going in our place of business for one reason or another, sometimes merely out of curiosity.

Some of the folks who dropped in on us from time to time were professional athletes with the Minnesota Twins and the Minnesota Vikings. We got acquainted with a lot of athletes through the business but at this time, I didn't spend much time watching football or baseball because I simply didn't have the leisure time to do so.

Anyway, this gentleman walked right up to me and said, "What's your name?"

"Name's Edgar Brooks," I replied, hardly glancing up from the duck I was mounting at the moment. "What's yours?" I may have been drinking a little at the time; I'm not sure.

211

"My name is Bud Grant," came the immediate response.

"Let's see, now," I said scratching my head; "Bud Grant. Seems like I've heard that name someplace..."

"Oh boy!" he barked. "Don't you have a television set?" I could see right off that this guy was a little ticked off with me. Small wonder, for I surely should have recognized both the name and the face of the head coach of the famous Minnesota Vikings football team!

Not long after that booboo on my part, the same thing occurred when Vern Gagne, who was the heavyweight wrestling champion of the world at the time, came into our shop for the first time. I failed to recognize who he was, just as I had fumbled the ball with Bud Grant. Remember my telling you how adept I was as a young boy at messin' up? Well, I guess it continued to be a characteristic of mine throughout my lifetime.

CATERING TO THE RICH AND FAMOUS

I little realized at the time I started putting together several audio tapes to be used by the author in writing this biography that I was opening floodgates of memories that had long been suppressed in the archives of my mind. Now, memories are flowing like the gushing discharge of water through raised gates in the locks on the Mississippi River between Minneapolis and St. Louis.

It has become self-evident in this venture that the more highly significant aspects of Allie's and my life, from early on to the present time, have more to do with the fantastic people that we have had the privilege of associating with

JOANNE CASTLE AND ALLIE BROOKS

than with the degree of success we may have experienced in our various enterprises.

To attempt to list the names of the many celebrities we have had occasion to do business with and in many instances, become personally acquainted with, would hardly be feasible. Suffice it to say that the list would include several presidents and vice-presidents of the United States, governors of several states, senators, representatives of state and federal political offices, along with a host of famous individuals from almost every walk of life. I sometimes have to pinch myself to determine if all this has actually happened to a back-woods guy who only went as far as the eighth grade in school, or if it is merely a fantastic dream. It all seems like a fantasy of drastic proportions.

Bob Allison and Bill Dailey, both with the Minnesota Twins, are two people who come to my mind at this moment. Both of them were frequent visitors in our taxidermy shop out in Columbia Heights. You may recall Bill Dailey's having been famous as a relief pitcher for the Twins some years back.

He and Bob Allison once gave Allie and me tickets to attend a Minnesota Twins game. It was at that particular ball game that Bill's pitching arm went bad. The Twins had been using him heavily in those days and he was winning a lot of games for them. I recall that he was sometimes concerned over the possibility of his overdoing it and throwing his arm out. Little did Allie or I know that we would be in the bleachers watching when it happened.

The club finally had to let Bill go. He couldn't even hold a spot in the minor leagues, his control of the ball got so bad. He was one mighty fine fellow and it was sad, indeed, for us to see it happen.

Another customer of ours was Les Kouba, the artist who painted duck stamps for the Government numerous times. Allie used to do the delicate tinting on the fish Les would bring in after fishing trips to various parts of the country.

Leon Boulanger, who played guitar in Ernest Tubb's band for many years, was a frequent visitor to our shop. I recall that oftentimes before the start of a given number, Ernest would say, "Play it pretty, Leon."

Being a member of Tubb's band called for Leon's having to be on the road much of the time. Leon's wife worked as a flight attendant, which also required her to be away from home a lot.

Because their respective lifestyles kept them apart so much of the time, Leon and his wife decided to give serious consideration to their getting into a different line of work that would enable them to live a more normal life together. So, Leon quit the band and his wife quit her job with the airline and he took over the parts department of a Buick garage in Minneapolis. I think the owner of the business was someone Leon knew quite well.

"Leon, would you consider teaching Allie and me to play a musical instrument?" I asked him one day.

"Sure," he said, "I'll be glad to."

All right," I continued, "you buy us a couple of guitars or whatever you think we'll need, and we'll start in."

Well, Leon bought each of us a big Standel guitar, along with an amplifier and some other paraphernalia and came out to the house to commence teaching us. We'd get to drinkin' and chewin' the fat about this and that and consequently didn't really get any serious lessons off the ground. They were fabulous instruments and we had them for a number of years before finally selling them after we eventually moved out of Minneapolis.

BALANCE OF NATURE

Somewhere along about this time, we got a letter from a fellow who lived in Des Moines by the name of Ed Ager. In his letter, he informed us that he owned 160 acres of land up on Buck Lake where Allie and I had spent our younger years. He wished to sell the land and wondered if we might, conceivably, be interested in buying it.

Allie and I drove up there at the first opportunity that presented itself and took a good look at it. While we were there, we decided to do some partridge hunting up in the vicinity of what was known as the Moose Lake Trail, about five miles north of Buck Lake. Several miles back in on that road, we came upon a bulldozer that belonged to my nephew. It was sitting there alongside the road near to where he was doing some logging. To our surprise, right behind that bulldozer stood a great big cow moose! Allie and I stopped and looked at it for awhile and pretty soon, the moose turned away and sauntered off into the woods with her calf following right on her heels.

We drove down the road about a quarter of a mile further and here stood another cow moose. This one had three calves with her! Now, I don't know if all of them belonged to her or not, because two of the calves were nice big ones and one was quite small. It might have been the off-spring of another cow that had died or it could have been a runt. I don't know. In any event, this big cow backed off the road a short distance and just stood there and looked at us. The calves sort of hid behind her and would peek around her to sneak a sly look at us every few minutes. We watched this moose cow and her calves for quite a while before driving on. As I recall, they were still standing there when we left.

We came back to Buck Lake, packed up our gear and went back to Minneapolis. In short order, we wrote Mr. Ager and purchased the entire 160 acres he wanted to sell. A little later, we put a travel trailer on the land, right near the spot where we eventually planned to build a home. When we felt the need to get away from the daily grind and stress in the taxidermy shop, we would slip up to our trailer to do some hunting and fishing, which has always been our first love for as far back as either of us can remember.

One time after we had moved back to Buck Lake permanently, I happened to look out of the big picture window of our house overlooking the lake, and here stood two big moose on the ice. In the winter, the lake freezes over solid enough to support several tons of weight without danger of breaking through.

This big bull moose and the cow that was with him had meandered on down to the lake out of the dense growth of trees nearby, just like they owned the place. Pretty soon, they nonchalantly walked back up onto the shore, ambled into a neighbor's yard and disappeared up through the driveway.

Another time, I observed a bunch of wolves out there on the ice eating a deer they had chased and eventually killed. I got pretty angry when I saw this happening and was sorely tempted to get the rifle out and do some shootin'. But timber wolves are now considered an endangered species and there is a $5,000 fine for shooting one.

Just why the hell wolves have been placed in the protected species category in this state, I can't imagine. The way it looks to me, pretty soon the deer that used to be so plentiful in northern Minnesota, will be in danger of becoming extinct and the wolves will be too plentiful.

It's a bit of a puzzle to me just why the government feels the need to encourage growth in the population of timber wolves. Now, I don't think they should be done away with completely, but I think they should use a little common sense in this matter.

There was a time when we would drive up to our resort on Lake Napoleon and see 25 deer on the road, and no timber wolves. Now, when we drive up that way, we see all kinds of timber wolves and very few deer. As I said, I wanted to get out my deer rifle and shoot every one of those wolves we saw eating that deer out on the lake, but the chance of someone living close by seeing me do this involved more risk than I felt I could afford to take.

That winter after we purchased the land from Mr. Ager, I was working in our shop there in Columbia Heights when suddenly, I found myself thinking about those moose calves Allie and I had seen earlier, wondering if some wolves would be bothering those calves.

I called Allie's brother, Auno Peratalo, who enjoyed the reputation of being one of the best wolf trappers in the entire Buck Lake area. Back in the old days, before we came to Minneapolis to live, Auno and I did a lot of trapping during the winter months.

I told him about the small moose calves Allie and I had seen earlier up on the Moose Lake Trail and expressed my concern as to whether or not the timber wolves were threatening their existence. Auno went up that way to have a look around and in a day or two I got a call from him.

"Did you find the calves?" I asked him.

"Yes, I found them," Auno answered, "and they're all dead. The timber wolves have killed all of them. There's one enormously large wolf amongst the pack that's running in this whole area. Why don't you come up and we'll have a closer look at this situation."

We drove up there and after checking things out, decided that Auno should set some traps and see what he could do. Then, we went on back to the Twin Cities.

Auno proceeded to set out his traps and carry out our plan. It was only a matter of days until he called and informed us that he had caught that big timber wolf. He had taken it into town and had it tagged and when they weighed the animal, it tipped the scales at 180 pounds!

180-POUND TIMBER WOLF TRAPPED BY AUNO PERATALO NEAR BUCK LAKE

Now, 180 pounds is thirty pounds more than any other timber wolf I've ever heard of anyone catching. There's one mounted and on display over at Bemidji, Minnesota, that weighs 150 pounds and that one has always been considered the largest ever.

We took pictures of this brute, which we still have in our large, loose-leaf scrapbook, showing Auno's big, full-grown Labrador retriever walking underneath that wolf's belly without touching it! Auno held the dead wolf carcass upright while the photo was being taken. That Lab weighed about 70 pounds, no small animal in its own right. In that same picture, is a big police dog standing there sniffin' the wolf's head. This police dog weighs about 85 or 90 pounds. In that enlarged photo, it can be clearly seen that the wolf's nose is about the same length as the police dog's entire head.

It was definitely the largest wolf I've ever seen, or ever will see in all probability. Why we didn't mount that animal, I'll never know. It's one of the biggest mistakes we ever made and I have kicked myself about that oversight ever since.

Auno skinned it out and sold the hide. Had we mounted it, we would have had a rare trophy in our possession, indeed.

Auno and I had been trapping partners when we had our resort up on Lake Napoleon. He would trap back in the hills and up in the high country along the rivers for wolves, lynx and bobcats, and I would trap the low ground for mink, otter and muskrat. Fisher had just moved into the area about the time we got through trapping, so we didn't catch many of them. We did succeed in getting a few, however. We also caught a lot of beaver during the beaver trapping season.

In the wintertime, when Auno and I were really into the trapping bit, it wasn't unusual for us to walk 25 miles on snowshoes on any given day. Now, that's a lot of walkin', in anybody's language!

If I were to try to do that today, they'd have to haul me out of the woods on a sled! I'd do good to make it about the first three miles or so and that would be the end of my trappin'.

When Auno and I were trapping together, we would cut holes in the ice and set our traps, through the ice, on the bottom. If we saw we had a beaver in the trap when we came along next time, we would cut out the hole again and pull the trapped beaver out through it. We would usually skin it right there on the ice. Sometimes, it would be 30 degrees below zero at the time. How our fingers ever stood that kind of temperature, I'll never know. Looking back, it's a wonder we didn't freeze to death, but it was the only way of life we knew, so we just went ahead and did it.

15

Escaping the drudgery

With the name "Brooks Taxidermy Service" now appearing regularly in most of the leading sports magazines and periodicals, and with the ever-escalating word-of-mouth advertising taking place on the part of sportsmen the world-over, we began to receive invitations from business organizations and affluent individuals to participate in hunting and fishing expeditions of every description imaginable. Invitations to go on African and Asian safaris presented themselves on several occasions, all of which we declined as graciously as we could. The time to set aside from our grueling daily grind simply wasn't available, or so we thought at the time.

Looking back on all this, we are keenly aware

that we passed up some golden opportunities to see remote parts of the world that, in all probability, we will never see. Some of these trips would have cost us thousands of dollars, were we to have assumed the cost ourselves.

We did, however, take advantage of several hunting and fishing trips, some of which were gestures of appreciation for some special favor we had done for customers. Some, too, were intended to entice us to consider taking on some sort of special taxidermy project, which in some instances involved hundreds, even thousands, of custom-designed mountings on plaques of various size and description. Some of these items were wanted for advertising purposes, some to hand out as gifts to select customers to whom gestures of good will were in order. To endeavor to include the details of all of these trips would assume the proportions of a telephone directory.

I might inject at this point, that one of the ongoing frustrations in our business was answering the telephone, which always seemed to ring just about the time we were up to our elbows in a particular operation that wasn't too easy to interrupt. There were times when I think it might have been feasible to have had our own PBX operator.

B-BAR-B BUFFALO RANCH

One day, I got a long distance telephone call from New York. A man by the name of Bud Basolo was inviting me to take a hunting trip to his ranch, which was located just south of Gillette, Wyoming. He wanted me to come out and hunt antelope.

I talked to him for awhile and finally said, "Bud, I'm going to have to take a rain check on it. When I do go hunting, usually in the fall, I hunt with my wife and daughter, uh..."

"Oh, that's okay," he replied, "bring your wife and daughter along. But don't come until you receive a formal invitation in the mail."

Within a relatively short period of time, a packet arrived containing our big game licenses, all paid for, and we were supposed to be out to Bud's ranch on a certain date.

I wondered just what the deal was on all this. I didn't have the slightest idea how he knew I even existed. When we finally got out there, we discovered that Bud's wife was a relative of someone in a San Francisco firm that did hide tanning for us. They had recommended us to do some taxidermy for Bud.

We managed to get our affairs in sufficient order to allow us to make the trip. When we arrived at Gillette, we drove south about 20 miles and finally came to a large stone gate with a high arch over it that read, "B-BAR-B Buffalo Ranch."

To our surprise, we were approached by several men who asked for our identification. It turned out that they were F.B.I. men and they were swarming all over the place! "What in hell are we getting into?" was the first thought that entered my head.

They let us through the gate and we traveled on down to the lodge. The next thing that caught my eye and aroused my curiosity even further was a fleet of 24 four-wheel drive trucks sitting there.

Allie, Marjorie and I alighted from our auto and walked into the lodge. Bud Basolo happened to be there at the time and we proceeded to exchange introductions. Mr. Basolo said, "Help yourselves to a drink, there." That's when we discovered that Bud ran a free liquor store right there at the lodge.

From around the first of September to the first of December or so, he invites around 40 guests at a time to come and hunt. He foots the whole bill for everything while they are there, including a free dining room, free liquor store, free locker plant service and free guide service.

When it's time to hunt, airplanes fly around his 60,000 acre ranch and spot the game. Then, the pilots let you know where the action is. Each of the four-wheel drive vehicles is driven by a guide, with only two passengers being allotted to each truck. When you get the message from the scout plane and drive to the location where you will be hunting, movie cameras are set up to film the action when you're doing your shooting—the whole bit, nothing left out.

Now, if you kill game and it is down in a deep canyon someplace, there are electric winches on these trucks that are used to retrieve your game for you. They back right up to the rim of the canyon, run a long cable down there and haul out your deer, antelope or whatever you may have shot.

When your game has been retrieved, they load it in the truck and take it to the locker plant and the next time you see this meat, it's all wrapped up in packages and frozen for you. The head is readied to be taken to a taxidermist and if you want it mounted, Bud will have it taken care of and sent to you. One hell of an operation, is the best way I know to describe it. The equal of which I've never seen before or since!

When we got ready to go hunting, Bud noticed our old Remington rifles and promptly suggested that each of us use one of his Weatherby rifles.

"No," I said, "these are okay. We'll do all right."

Before it was over with, all three of us, Marjorie, Allie and I, had shot a deer and an antelope apiece. We never missed a one. When it came time for Bud to use his Weatherby rifle, he missed four shots in a row and amiably informed us that he wished he had kept his mouth shut about our preference in rifles.

Now, when we started to put on a drive for these antelope, an airplane would fly in close behind them and drive them toward us. I got situated on my designated stand and was all ready to do some shooting when I heard the airplane coming in the distance.

"Edgar," Bud had advised me on our way out to where we would be hunting, "when you see those antelope comin', you lead them twice the length of the running animal."

"Oh, boy!" I thought. "I've done enough hunting to know better than that!"

I soon learned there is a vast difference between shooting wild game out in the vast open spaces of Wyoming and shooting wild game in the bush country of northern Minnesota. Distance is deceptive out in that area.

The first drive got underway and soon, here came the antelope, being relentlessly pursued by that airplane. I picked out a buck, took a shot at him...and killed the doe behind him! I couldn't believe it!

"My God," I thought, "that was a funny deal!"

A second drive was started and the same thing happened to me that had happened the first time. So, I decided it might be a good idea to heed Bud Basolo's instructions to shoot twice the length ahead of a running animal, even if it was something I had never heard of before.

On the third drive, here came a beautiful buck. This time, I led him by two lengths and sure enough, I killed him. Now, I stated a little earlier that none of the three of us missed one shot using our old Remington rifles in preference to Bud's Weatherbys. I should have said that this was so, but only after I had learned the hard way to follow my host's advice.

Now, before the gang left the lodge to go hunting, lunch buckets were packed for each of us, 40 of them. Not only did their contents consist of a variety of food, but each bucket contained a fifth of gin, a fifth of vodka and a fifth of brandy!

When we would stop at noon to eat, a drink was had with everybody and all of us would visit for a spell. When someone succeeded in shooting a game animal, each one would have a drink around. Now that was all fine and good, but...don't go too far with it. If anyone became inebriated while out hunting, that was the end of his hospitable invitation to be a guest at Bud's ranch!

Now, once you have been invited, you are permanently on Bud's guest list and you can go there every year. I didn't go out there a second time, for reasons you might accurately speculate upon. It was a little too much for me. I couldn't take all of it in stride.

In due time, Bud let it be known to the three of us just why we had gotten this unexpected invitation to come out to his ranch. Bud wanted us to make up 900 buffalo foot ashtrays that he wished to give to his friends. Through selective breeding over a period of years, Bud Basolo had developed a herd of more than 2,000 first-rate bison. This lacked only 800 of equaling the entire buffalo holdings of the United States Government on its various refuges. We learned at this time, also, that his large herd of buffalo was used in the filming of the movie "How The West Was Won." So, this was how Bud Basolo had such a large number of buffalo feet on hand for the ashtrays he wanted made.

It became my unpleasant duty to inform our gracious host that there was simply no way we could consider undertaking a project of this size at that time. Our pressing circumstances just wouldn't allow it.

When or if you were permitted to shoot one of his buffalo, Bud would have the head mounted and sent to you free of charge and he asked me to take 44 buffalo heads back to Minneapolis to mount. Again, I had to refuse his request. There simply was no way we could do it.

Bud's ranch was used frequently for making movies, I understand. The old ranch house appears in some of them, as do his buffalo. Shortly after our time there, a movie film was being made at the ranch. During the filming, Quintin Marcus, who was our guide, was flying his plane straight up into the air when the engine conked out on him. The plane came down and Quintin was killed in the crash. I had mailed Quintin some mounted pheasants and some other stuff to put in his home for decorations, but I think he died before they arrived.

Something that impressed us immensely about Bud Basolo was the man's down-to-earth, unpretentious way of operating. When we first arrived at his ranch, we thought he might prove to be one of the well-dressed gentlemen to be seen most everywhere on the ranch. But no, Bud turned out to be the fellow dressed in a pair of western togs all smeared over with grease and blood.

Bud had a locker plant out on his ranch that was larger than any locker plant I've ever seen in Minneapolis. When we'd get up to go out hunting in the morning, Bud could be seen out there cutting up meat, which we found out was his trade. Butchering meat had played an integral part in his having achieved a laudable degree of affluence after leaving the Merchant Marines following World War II.

We have a feature article that appeared in *The True Man's Magazine* tucked away in our large scrapbook. This lengthy article, written by Rufus Jarman, divulges in detail the fantastic story of Bud's early beginnings as a meat cutter working for $50 a week, to the attainment of his present prestigious position in the business world.

Sensing the possibilities in developing a market for buffalo meat, Bud proceeded to promote the sale of this product through such sizable outlets as the Safeway stores around the country. This venture played the foremost role in his eventually purchasing the huge ranch he now owns.

The B-BAR-B Buffalo Ranch had about everything you could imagine, including its private fire department, consisting of the cutest little red fire truck you've ever seen.

Even Bud's approach to maintaining his fleet of four-wheel drive trucks was a bit unusual. Due to the rough terrain they were constantly being driven over, those trucks took quite a beating. Bud's practice was to replace any truck as soon as it had 10,000 miles on it. The garage would just bring out a new one and take the old one away. Nothing more was said about it and no questions were asked. There wasn't much one could think of that had been overlooked in Bud's operation.

Not long after we had been out there, I got a letter from the Texas Meat Growers Association.

On the letterhead appeared the name D.C. Basolo, Jr., President. Later, I received a letter from the Denver Meat Packers. Guess what! On the letterhead appeared the name D.C. Basolo, Jr., President! Still another time, I got a letter from Safeway Foods, out on the west coast. As with the others, the letterhead displayed the name D.C. Basolo, Jr., President.

I was told that when Bud was hitchhiking home after his discharge from the Merchant Marines, flat broke, he was given a ride by a traveling salesman. This fellow sparked the idea from which Bud's spectacular success evolved. He has built his fortune all on his own, as far as I know.

We heard that his wife and possibly his father induced him to retire at one point in his life. He gave retirement a try but it wasn't compatible with his ambitious nature. He'd go downtown San Francisco and maybe run into some friends who were somewhat down on their luck at the time, so he would invite a bunch of them out to his ranch and show them a good time.

He had waitresses there to serve his guests and about everything in the way of creature comforts one could imagine. And when his guests were about to leave, he'd insist upon filling their cars with gas! I once tried to come up with some vague idea of what all this was costing the guy. I figured it must be costing him somewhere in the area of $5,000 a day to entertain his friends out there.

After we had been out there, one thing that kept bugging me was what the reason might have been for all those F.B.I. agents to be on the scene, ridin' the fences all night long and generally watching over the place. About a month or so after we got back home, we saw on television where there had been a cancer test conducted on a buffalo farm someplace, which hadn't turned out quite as favorably as they had hoped. I have wondered, since, whether Bud Basolo's buffalo ranch was involved in that occurrence.

At the time of our arrival at the B-BAR-B Buffalo Ranch, President Lyndon Johnson and Robert McNamara, his Secretary of Defense, were just leaving. Bing Crosby, Nat King Cole and his daughter, Natalie, who became a popular singer in her own right in more recent years, were also there. Natalie visited the Basolos out at the ranch quite frequently, we were told. And when the Brooks tribe arrived, those timber savages from Buck Lake brought the quality of guests up considerably, y'know!

After we got back home, I wondered what I could do to show our appreciation of Bud Basolo's generous and graciously-tendered hospitality while we were guests at his ranch. So, I called one of the Arctic fishing camps I was familiar with and asked them what the chances were of bringing Bud up on a fishing trip. I explained who he was and what he was. I was assured that, not only were they interested in having him come up, but there would be no charge. "Just get him up here," they said.

I wrote Bud a letter and asked him if he would like to go to the Arctic on a fishing trip, but he declined. He didn't savor the idea of someone's paying for his way.

During our conversation, several items of interest emerged. I learned that when colder weather arrived in Wyoming and there was snow on the ground, he used specially-built vehicles with half-tracks on them, enabling the guides to get where they wanted to go under conditions that otherwise would prove impossible.

I also learned that Bud owned a home right next to Bing Crosby's in Beverly Hills at that time. Bud Basolo stands out as an impressive example of how far one can go in life if the will to succeed is strong enough, especially here in the United States of America. As to his venture into retirement, I dare say it was undoubtedly short-lived. I'm willing to bet anyone a $5 bill that on any given day at the B-BAR-B Buffalo Ranch south of Gillette, you'll find Bud Basolo, decked out in his blood-stained western togs, cuttin' up buffalo meat out in his locker plant. That's what he was doing when I saw him last and that's the way I want to remember him.

YOU'VE GOT ULCERS

Over the years, some of the larger, more prestigious hunting and fishing camps around the world became aware of the goodly number of celebrities who had become our regular customers. Apparently, they had figured out that catering to Brooks Taxidermy Service of Minneapolis, Minnesota was one of the best ways to establish contacts and business relationships with this caliber of prospective customer.

Nearly every week, we were receiving invitations to visit various camps across the country. A preponderance of these were from the Arctic area, so Allie and I started to take advantage of the opportunity to fish in that remote part of the world. One of our favorite spots was Great Bear Lake. Occasionally, we would tear ourselves away from our ever-existent workload in the shop and go up there for a week or so at a time. Sometimes when we'd come back, I could scarcely remember that we had been there or what we had been doing while we had been away!

Life was becoming a terrible nightmare for me. With all those fish coming in to be mounted, I began to rely more and more heavily on booze to help me keep going. I was becoming more irritable and nervous with each passing day.

Sometimes, I would go upstairs into the front room and just sit there by myself in my lounge chair for a spell. If this didn't do it, I would draw a tub of hot water and soak in it as long as it took for me to get my act together a little better. And, of course, I generally included a generous intake of hard liquor as part of the "therapy." I hadn't quite come to the place where I could face the fact that the stress and booze were slowly, but inexorably, killing me.

"Edgar," my wife said to me one day, "you're going to the hospital."

"Allie," I responded, defensively, "there's nothing that hospital is going to do for me. Nerves and alcohol are doin' me in and I don't think hospitals can do anything for that."

Allie stood her ground and reluctantly, I went over to the Northwestern Memorial Hospital in Minneapolis. The first thing they did was draw several vials of blood from my arm. They drew so much blood out of me that I commenced to wonder if they were starting a new blood bank, or perhaps were availing themselves of some inexpensive anti-freeze! This went on for quite a while. Finally, they stuck me in bed and started giving me barium. Have you ever tasted barium? It's worse than some of that bottom-shelf booze! Terrible stuff!

I remained in the hospital for a week or 10 days. Not once was alcohol mentioned by the doctors examining me. Finally, one morning, a

232

little doctor came racing in with a pronouncement.

"Edgar," he said, "we've found the trouble."

"What's the matter with me, anyway?" I asked him.

"You've got ulcers."

"Oh, ho!" I said. "Now that's exactly what I thought I had when I came in here. What do we do about that?"

"I'm going to give you a prescription for some pills, which I want you to go home and take. You stick with taking these and adhere to the diet I'm going to put you on, and I'm quite certain you're going to be all right."

"I'm sure you're right, doctor," I said. "Give me that stuff, I'm going home."

He gave me my diet list and all those pills and I checked out. I went home and tossed the whole shebang in the garbage pail. I didn't any more have ulcers than the man in the moon! I knew full-well what my problem was by this time but as I said, alcohol wasn't mentioned once all the time I was in there.

Well, one good thing had resulted from my bein' in that hospital: It had gotten me away from the crowd long enough that I was starting to feel some better. I went back to work and the fish and the African game started pourin' in again as heavy as always.

Custom work

Shortly after I had gotten back into the harness again, a minister by the name of Reverend Salto came into the shop. Now, Reverend Salto and Governor Youngdahl were the two people who put the slot machines out of Minnesota. It had been quite a battle and he had scars to show for it, too.

The Reverend had 2,700 pounds of horns and hides from Africa that he wanted mounted. He had elephant feet to be made into ash trays, elephant ears that he wanted made into curtains for his recreation room windows, tusks that he wanted prepared to hang over the wider doors, leopards, and just about any animal you could name.

We worked on this order for a long, long time—several years, all told, as I recall. We had to squeeze it in along with our inflow of business as best we could. When we had completed the job for Reverend Salto, he had one of the nicest trophy display rooms that one could imagine.

Every time we felt the volume and tempo of our business had surely reached its saturation limit, some new and totally unanticipated dimension of patronage would thrust itself upon us. Somehow, God only knows how, we always managed to sandwich it into our fixed schedules.

We began to get more calls to do custom taxidermy work and to help design trophy display rooms for individuals and business firms. These special requests got to be an awful load on all of us. There were people running in and out of the place, the doorbell was ringing almost constantly and the phone was ringing off the wall. How I managed to get through all this without going totally insane, I'll never know.

Along about this time, a man came into the shop with a special request. Plans were underway to enter Jackie Robinson into the Major League Baseball Hall of Fame. This new arrival at our shop had been delegated to see if we could make up two nice pheasants to present to

Jackie at that occasion. Of course, we considered it an honor to be selected to do this job. We mounted the pheasants and they turned out real nice. That's been a number of years ago, but remains one of the memorable happenings in our lives.

BUSH PILOT

During the time we were operating the shop in Columbia Heights and living in St. Anthony, a fellow by the name of Dewey Smith contacted us. He operated an electrical shop on Highway 18, between Ventura and Clear Lake, Iowa. Dewey was planning a trip to the Arctic to hunt polar bear and wanted to know if we could mount his bear for him if and when he got one.

"I should warn you, Mr. Smith," I told him, "it's pretty hard to bring a polar bear back from up there. Those guides get 15 percent commission if they ship the bear to certain taxidermy shops up there."

"Don't worry about that," Dewey responded, "I'll get mine out of there O.K. Never fear."

So Dewey killed a big polar bear and contacted us with the information as to when he would be arriving at the Minneapolis Airport. Allie and I were waiting there for him when he arrived.

"Edgar, I got my polar bear and got it to the plane," he said when he had alighted from the incoming flight, "and just as you said, the pilot wanted to know what taxidermist I was planning to send it to. When I informed him I was taking it to Brooks Taxidermy in Minneapolis, he said, "No, no, we've got taxidermists right up here that we send them to.""

Dewey insisted he was going to bring it to us and that pilot left him stranded right there on the ice with his polar bear! Somehow or another, probably with the help of his wife, who had stayed in Anchorage, he got another pilot by the name of Jack Lee to come up and get him.

Jack Lee was a guide from Anchorage who specialized in grizzly bear hunting for the most part. One time he took a man hunting up there and from the airplane, they saw a bear go into a clump of tag-alder. They landed the plane just close enough to where they had spotted the bear so as not to spook him.

"Now, you stay right behind me with your gun," Jack instructed his hunter. "I'm going to walk ahead. When I see that grizzly, I'm going to duck down and you shoot right over the top of me."

So, Jack got the bear's attention, all right, and it headed right for them. Jack ducked down, but didn't hear any shooting. When he looked around, the guy behind him was runnin' in the opposite direction, gun and all, as fast as his legs could carry him!

That grizzly came onto Jack Lee and ripped him up badly, even tore some of his insides out. Somehow, someone managed to get him to a hospital. He was in bad shape, but he lived through the traumatic ordeal. Those bush pilots up there are something else, believe me. They take their lives in their hands every time they take someone out hunting.

MIXED UP FISH

Another fishing trip to the Arctic that I'll never forget had its inception when we received a telephone call from Colonel Sanders' group in Las Vegas, Nevada. They knew Allie and I were fishing the Arctic quite a bit and they asked if we could accompany them on a fishing trip they were planning to take in that region.

Well, let me tell you sumthin'; when you go fishing with Colonel Sanders' group (that's Kentucky Fried Chicken, you know), you know you've been on a fishing trip!

We took a big four-motor plane out of the Twin Cities and headed for Winnipeg, Canada. When we arrived at Winnipeg, one of the motors on our plane was acting up, necessitating an unscheduled stop-over while they got the engine repaired or replaced, I don't remember which now. In any event, we were told we would be departing the following morning.

They got the motor business taken care of but when it came time to go, we couldn't find the Colonel Sanders' bunch anywhere. We looked all over for them and finally found them in somebody's hotel room. They were playing poker, imbibing alcoholic beverages and having themselves a good time! We got them all rounded up and on the plane and headed for Great Bear Lake up in the Arctic.

As we were preparing to land, I looked down at the little sandy airstrip they were going to land this big four-motor plane on and I thought, "Boy! We've had it for sure, now!" This may have been Allie's and my last trip to Great Bear Lake, I'm not sure.

They didn't seem to have any problem making a safe landing and pretty soon, we saw several boats coming to take us to our destination. It was sometime in July when we arrived, and we were chagrined to find Great Bear Lake completely frozen over. Our fishing had to be done in rivers and obscure coves, instead. It seemed a little late in the year for the lake to be frozen and I expressed my displeasure to the operators of our camp at their not having notified us of this possibility ahead of time.

When all of us got properly situated, they rented two smaller planes to haul us around. The Sanders' party used one of them and another bunch of us used the other one. One day when we were flying across Great Bear Lake, a door on that cussed plane flew open! I'll tell you, it scared everybody half to death!

"Don't pay any attention to that, it does that every once in awhile," the pilot assured us. Those bush pilots are fabulous pilots. They can get in and out of places most people would think to be impossible.

Over the years in our taxidermy business, we had encountered a puzzling problem, and we chanced upon the reason for it while on this trip. From time to time we would mount a fish for someone and send it out to them. Then we'd get a letter back to the affect that there was something they couldn't understand—their fish had grown four inches or some such matter. I couldn't figure how this could possibly happen because I was making a plaster cast of every fish I worked on and knew the exact size. One day, I chanced to open some freezer doors while we were there on this trip with the Sanders' group and observed a goodly number of fish that were tagged, "Trophy Unknown."

They were just shipping trophy-caliber fish without going to any great lengths to make sure the right people were getting the fish they had actually caught. Allie lost one of hers before we got on the plane to return home, due to erroneous tagging. When we got back to Winnipeg, our fish weren't to be found amongst the stuff that was coming up the escalator. Come to find out, a group of stockholders, who were at the camp at the same time we were, got all of our fish.

Most of our fish were smoked fish, being brought back to eat, but everyone in the group brought back one fish each to have us mount. The smallest of these weighed 35 pounds, the largest one tipped the scales at 52 pounds. There were 11 of these fish in all. Let me tell you, that's a nice string of fish to cast your eyes upon. The Arctic produces some fabulous fish and we have had the opportunity to see our share of them.

ONE DAY AT A TIME

It was difficult to find taxidermists who were capable of doing the quality of work consistent with the reputation we had built. I could hire all kinds of people to handle the rough work but at that time, it was almost impossible to find anyone to do finish work. There are more good taxidermists around the country today than there were back then, I'm happy to say.

If we would leave the place for any period of time, we would always find a large accumulation of finish work awaiting us when we returned. So there was always a feeling of drudgery that accompanied our return from a vacation of any kind, due to this inevitable work load staring us in the face.

We were living in the house in St. Anthony and trying our best to get some room cleared away in our house over on Central Avenue, but meeting with little success in any such endeavor. From time to time, Allie and I would seriously discuss getting out of the business entirely before both of us wound up with a serious breakdown in our health. Of course, my problem with booze was creating more prospects for this happening to me than to Allie, who was hanging in there better than I, fortunately.

We thought some relief was in the offing with Mr. Ager, the man from whom we had purchased the 160 acres of land up at Buck Lake. He expressed interest in buying into our business and eventually, he bought Marjorie's share of the business and began working with us in the shop. It didn't take him too long to realize that he had bit off more than he cared to chew, so we bought back his equity in the business. A bit later, a nephew of mine, who was in the taxidermy business in Washington, bought into our business. That didn't last long either. So the hopes we had for our being able to relax a bit, turned sour once again.

Along about this time, Marjorie got married and moved to Missouri. She opened up a taxidermy shop down there and did all of our rug work—lions, tigers, zebras, bears. She made rugs from the hides of every wild animal one might mention, in addition to her own regular taxidermy work. I used to go down once in awhile in the winter and help her a little. That was always a fun time for both of us.

Not having Marjorie with us in our Minneapolis operation now created a vacuum that Allie and I were keenly aware of every day we opened up the shop for business. Not only had she filled the role of bookkeeper and business advisor in difficult decisions that were constantly arising, but Marjorie could always be counted upon to hold up her end in our assembly-line operation.

Allie and I found some consolation in the old cliche, "We've lost a daughter, but we've gained a son-in-law." In due time, two grandsons, Keith and Kelly, came along and we assumed the role of proud grandparents.

KELLY, KEITH & MARJORIE KITCHEN; ALLIE BROOKS, EARL KITCHEN & EDGAR BROOKS

We kept hangin' in there as best we could. The lyrics of the popular song "One Day at a Time" became our own private theme song as we faced each new day. But as the days, weeks and months slid by, we slowly began to face the vivid reality that our endurance was limited.

I had two hunting trips to Africa offered me by people who not only wanted me to accompany them, but who were willing to pay all of my expenses, which customarily amounted to around $10,000 per person.

I didn't go on either one of them! I was either too busy, too tired or perhaps more accurately stated, too dumb to take advantage of such a rare opportunity.

"There'll be another day, another opportunity," I told myself, but that day and opportunity never recurred.

"Allie," I addressed my wife one day, at a time when I was feeling the burden of a myriad of pressing responsibilities heavily, "we've got to take the bull by the horns and start making concrete plans to get out of the taxidermy business. I'm not going to be able to keep on going like this much longer. I think I'm slowly but surely losing my mind. It has finally gotten to be entirely too much for both of us."

We had this large parcel of land up at Buck Lake that we had purchased earlier, so we decided to find us a good carpenter to build a house up there on our property. We got in touch with a fellow from Chicago who had a reputation for being about the best house builder to be found anywhere.

George proved himself to be a fabulous carpenter and we were well-pleased with the quality of his workmanship, but his wife eventually became lonesome for their children and homesick, too, I suspect. She prevailed upon her husband to conclude the project and return to Chicago. The poor fellow finally acquiesced to her wishes and went back, leaving us with much of the interior finish work yet to be completed.

We sold our house in Columbia Heights to a chiropractor in Minneapolis and set a date for us to be moved out, enabling the new owner to move in. We continued to live in the house in St. Anthony until we disposed of it and moved back to Buck Lake.

The
Golden
Years

16

Return to Buck Lake

We had planned to have the new house finished before we moved, which would have provided us with the necessary space for the large inventory of as yet unfinished taxidermy items, our taxidermy equipment, our household furniture and our personal belongings. Now, with our carpenter's abandoning us and leaving us with gobs of work to be done, we were faced with a new and vexing dilemma: We would have to finish the interior work ourselves! So, here we were, trying to escape the stress and strain we had been saddled with for 20 years and finding ourselves in a situation that was resulting in more, not less, stress!

What remained to be done consisted of laying

up the stone fireplace between the dining room and the living room, putting in the breakfast nook, putting the cupboards up, laying the floor tile, and trimming out the woodwork.

Now, Allie and I had gotten lots of experience in this sort of thing when we built the cabins at our summer resort on Napoleon Lake prior to our moving to Minneapolis. Lacking the know-how needed to finish the interior of the house wasn't our problem. The problem lay in the fact that all this was going to have to be accomplished by working around all the stuff we would have to bring back with us from Minneapolis.

In addition to our large inventory of deer-feet gun racks, deer-feet lamps and deer-feet foot stools piled high in whatever space we could allocate for storage, we had to find room for our taxidermy equipment and our household goods.

We hauled everything from Minneapolis up to our new, partially-completed house at Buck Lake and piled it up wherever we could find a place for it. It took some doing, but we were able to vacate the Minneapolis houses on the respective dates that had been agreed upon.

With this accomplished, Allie and I tied into the monumental task confronting us. Not only did we face the major project of finishing the interior of the new house, but we had 480 frozen fish waiting to be processed and delivered to their owners.

It goes without saying that, between those two objectives, we burned a lot of midnight oil for quite a spell. We would empty one room and finish it and then we'd move everything that was stacked up in the next room into the one we had just finished, and go to work on the next one.

Finishing the interior work would have been a real challenge if we could have done it while it was still empty, but having to constantly shuffle all this stuff from one place to another made the job doubly difficult, not to mention irritating.

Tempers flared a'plenty before we commenced to see some daylight at the end of what seemed like a long, dark tunnel. Our hoped-for shortcut to some degree of retirement from the rat-race was now proving itself to be the damndest mess we had ever gotten ourselves into, and we had encountered some dillies!

We had sort of envisioned just slipping quietly away from Minneapolis and "riding off into the sunset," as in the ending scenario of an old western movie. Boy! What a rude awakening we were in for before we finally got ourselves squared around and settled into the old haunts where our younger years had been spent.

If there is one thing that might be said more than anything else in all this, it is that Allie and I are survivors. The instinct of survival is an inherent legacy that we both possess in abundance.

Now during all this, I found myself laboring under as much or more of a nervous strain than I had been while in Minneapolis and it was driving me nuts! My older brother, George, helped us a lot in getting the house finished and that took off some of the pressure.

In due time, the building project was completed and when the last nail had been driven and the final coat of varnish applied to the woodwork, Allie and I sort of stepped back and overviewed our handiwork with a measure of pride.

But I made one hell of a mistake; I forgot to put seat belts on the furniture! My drinking had increased in direct proportion to the intensity of the building project. Sometimes, I'd wake up on the floor, sometimes down in the basement, sometimes in the bathtub.

Have you ever woke up in the bathtub with your hard hat on and fully dressed in your snowmobile suit and boots? Well, I have and believe me, it's a weird feeling to look around you and see that big white receptacle all around you with no cover...it looks like a coffin.

WALK THE SECOND MILE

Now, when we finally pulled down the curtain on our taxidermy operation in Minneapolis, we hadn't really put out any word as to where we were going. It was our intention to finish the stuff we had on hand, and call it quits. If my memory serves me correctly, we were nearly eight years getting those 480 fish processed that we kept frozen in our deep freezers in the basement.

With our new home now finished, Allie and I

would mount as many of these fish as we could load in our pick-up truck and drive down to Minneapolis. We would rent a motel room and contact our customers who had been patiently waiting for their mounted fish and they would come and pick up their stuff.

Somehow, the word leaked out where we were now living. No sooner had we begun to make pretty good headway on our backlog of fish, when new business started finding its way to our door. By the time we had worked our way through that pile of frozen fish, we found ourselves just about as far away from being able to retire as we had been in Minneapolis!

One of the factors that played a large part in the reputation Brooks Taxidermy Service had earned over the years was Allie's expertise in getting the colors of the mounted fish as close to their original color as possible.

Somewhere along the line, we began to get landlocked salmon into the shop for mounting, in addition to the more customary species of fish that had been coming to us. We began encountering some criticism as to the coloring not being exactly as these critics felt it should be. This was something we weren't used to and it disturbed us no little bit. So, we decided to go up to Reindeer Lake, where these landlocked salmon were being caught, and try to determine for ourselves what we were doing wrong.

We trolled back and forth through a hole that wasn't more than 200 feet in diameter and caught nine landlocked salmon and would you believe, there weren't any two of them the same color!

Then, we came up with an idea that held some promise for helping solve the coloring problem. We decided to have the fishermen take colored photographs of their catch for us to go by when finishing the trophies. John Appleby, from jolly ol' England, had always taken his own private photographer along with him on his fishing excursions up to the Arctic. In mounting his fish, we always had something concrete to work on in getting the coloring right. His idea now helped us solve the problem of satisfying our landlocked salmon customers.

Another species of fish we encountered some coloring problems with was Arctic char. Arctic char coming from Tree River are red halfway up. From Victoria Island, they look like goldfish in color, orange all the way up. From the Inmin River, they are pretty much silver-colored. All in all, there were about six different colors to contend with when processing Arctic char. The trick was to know exactly where they had been caught, so as to know just how to get the colors acceptably correct.

Although we were still intent on retiring from taxidermy work, at least the heavy volume, we couldn't bring ourselves to compromise the quality of our work. We couldn't allow these coloring problems to become a sour note as we left a business that had been built on doing our level best to please our customers.

Being willing to "walk the second mile," to quote a passage from the Sermon on the Mount in the Bible, had sort of been our trademark during our years in business. Pursuing this ideal paid off in more ways than one. Not only did it reward us with moderate monetary success, but it left us an even greater legacy—a clear conscience.

An incident comes to mind that exemplifies how fussy some of these big-time sportsmen can be. One day I got a long-distance phone call from Detroit, Michigan. This fellow told me he had been fishing up in Tree River for Arctic char. He had run across a doctor from Minneapolis who had told him, "By all means, send that Arctic char to Brooks Taxidermy if you want it to be the right color."

"Can I get you to mount this char for me?" he inquired on the phone. Apparently, he had gotten wind of the fact that we weren't exactly soliciting new business.

"We'll be glad to," I assured him.

"What's the best way to get it to you?" he rejoined.

"Put it in a box and pack it good with dry ice. Mark it, 'Perishable, Please Rush,' and take it to United Parcel Service for shipment. Monday is a preferable day to ship it to avoid the possibility of weekend delays." He assured me that is what he would do.

The following day, I got a call from him informing me that the total weight of the crate, after it had been readied for shipment, was 109 pounds!

"U.P.S. won't accept that heavy parcel. I'm going to have to send it by Air Express," the fellow from Detroit informed me. "Now here's what we'll do: I'm going to put this crated fish on a plane and every time this plane lands between here and you, you're going to know about it." So, here is a little nine-pound Arctic char in a crate that now weighs 109 pounds coming in by Air Express!

The following day we got a call from Chicago saying, "We have a fish here from Mr. so-and-so. It has arrived at the air terminal here in Chicago and we're going to ship it to Minneapolis now." They seemed to know all about this fellow, whoever he was.

Pretty soon, we got a call from an official at the Minneapolis Terminal informing us that Mr.

so-and-so's fish had arrived and that they were going to forward it by air to Hibbing. They told us what time it should arrive and that we would be notified when it did.

A relatively short time later, we got a call from the Hibbing Airport.

"We've got a crated fish here from some guy in Detroit and it says on the label that it is to be delivered to you by cab if that's possible," the man on the phone informed us.

Just about then, a neighbor walked in and told us he was going to drive over to Hibbing for some reason. I phoned the airport at Hibbing immediately and told them I had a neighbor coming over there at such and such a time and that he would pick up this fish and bring it to us.

"Boy, is that a relief to me," the fellow on the phone retorted. "This guy is some V.I.P. there in Detroit, and we surely don't want anything bad to happen to it. I'll be glad to get it off my hands!"

We got that nine-pound Arctic char mounted and sent back to Detroit, following the same procedures to return it as he had insisted upon in getting it to us. This was only one of the many cases where people, who had obviously spent a lot of money going up to the Arctic or to Africa or wherever, didn't seem to mind spending whatever it happened to cost to have the assurance that their taxidermy work was going to be done just right.

The closer we got to a tentative retirement date, the busier we got. When we did finally get around to retiring, we almost had to hire a helper to help us accomplish it.

We moved back to Buck Lake on May 3, 1973, and spent nearly eight years getting

THIS GRIZZLY STANDS HEAD AND SHOULDERS ABOVE 6-FOOT TALL BRUCE KRUGER

caught up with the backlog of fish we brought from Minneapolis. We were another five years getting things tapered down to a point where we could live with it. New business trickled in from time to time and still does to this day. But it doesn't work a hardship on us. It's mostly taken on as an accommodation for friends.

FRIENDS IN HIGH PLACES

In the spring of 1979, a fellow by the name of Jeff Perrella, for whom we have done a lot of taxidermy work and who is a part owner of the

Sammy's Pizza & Restaurant chain, stopped in at our taxidermy shop at Buck Lake.

Jeff was a close friend of Walter Mondale, vice president of the United States at the time. He went on to explain that Vice President Mondale had expressed a desire to stay with Allie and me for awhile and fish a lake that was located about 14 miles north of where we lived.

Allie and I were quite excited about this matter at first, but after digging into it a little deeper, we found out that the vice president would have to have his full staff of 23 people along with him.

Well, this left us out. We simply didn't have enough room to accommodate this sizable entourage. Nonetheless, we felt highly honored to have been selected as possible hosts for Walter Mondale on his fishing trip. It isn't every day that people get the opportunity to entertain the vice president of the United States of America!

17

Elixir of life

About seven years after our return to Buck Lake, I began to come under conviction concerning my drinking. I began to decide I'd had about enough of that monkey on my back, which I now realized it had become.

"Allie," I addressed my wife one day, "I think I'm going to try to quit my drinkin'. I'm going to get in touch with Alcoholics Anonymous (A.A.)."

"Edgar," Allie replied, "you've tried everything else and nothing seemed to work. I have my doubts that this will either."

"Well, I don't have any assurance that it will, but I don't know what else to do. I'm going to give it a try."

I called A.A. and they sent two people out to talk to me. Now, up to this point, I had never met the Lord personally, but when those two people walked in the door, I think I came as close to meeting the Lord as I ever will. I think these people probably saved my life.

They sat down and talked to me most of that afternoon. They told me about a meeting that was going to be held downtown and if I would come to this meeting, they thought they could give me some help.

I went down to this meeting and was quite impressed with what I saw there. Now, when I walked through that door to attend that meeting, a miracle of some sort took place. I have never had a desire to drink booze again from that moment to now! I don't know what happened to me, but the desire for liquor was taken from me once and for all, right then and there.

They encouraged me to come back to more meetings in the future, which I did. They told me they thought I should have a sponsor. Since everything else they had told me had proven to be truthful, I got myself a sponsor—a farmer who lived out north of Nashwauk.

This farmer was a wonderful fellow, dedicated to the A.A. Program. He was used to dealing with dumb animals and I have always thought this was the reason he was so darned successful with me!

LIABILITY TURNED ASSET

Well, things went along. I began to heal up and things began to get better. I commenced speaking around the country to various groups. I would speak at the Hibbing hospital every once in a while. I have spoken at the prison in Sandstone a few times and I've spoken at Moose Lake Regional Treatment Center a few times.

There came a time when Allie's back commenced acting up again and she had to go back to Rochester. Just before we left Buck lake for Rochester, I got a call from Seattle, Washington. There was a girl out there who was going into treatment in the A.A. program and they wondered if I would make an audio tape for her. They thought maybe listening to the tape might help her.

"Boy, that sounds like a good thing," I thought. "While I'm waiting for Allie in the hospital there at Rochester, I'll be able to make this tape and kind of pass the time away."

In about three days in the privacy of my hotel room, I had the tape finished. I took it down to the front desk to mail it out and told the desk clerk what it was.

"Are you one of us?" he asked me forthrightly. His question took me by surprise.

"What do you mean, 'Are you one of us?'" I replied.

"Are you in the program?" he inquired.

"I sure am," I affirmed.

"Well, isn't that a miracle," he reiterated. "I am, too! By the way, we're having a meeting over at the Alamo Club. Would it be possible for you to come over there and speak to us?"

"Well," I said, "I'm not very well prepared, but I'm honored to be given such an opportunity while I'm down here at Rochester," which I was.

About three nights later, I got a chance to speak to another group in Rochester. Then, soon thereafter, I was solicited to speak to yet a third group. Once again, as had happened so many times to me from early on, I was finding the direction of my life being ushered into new routes that were least expected. I was finding it necessary to accept and adapt myself to new dimensions in my lifestyle that I had unknowingly been prepared to enter by forces my finite mind will never fully comprehend. But suddenly, here I was, now filling the role of a counselor for those standing in need of being delivered from alcohol addiction, when only a short time prior to this, it was I who was desperately seeking help for the same affliction.

"Y'know, it's somewhat of a paradox," I would tell them. "They told me up in northern Minnesota before I left, that if and when I came down here, there would be people who could tell me how to take care of my health and overall well-being. Now, here I am telling people how to take care of their health. So, it really seems to have been somewhat of a miracle that has taken place."

There will never be any doubt in my mind, whatsoever, that I was the beneficiary of a miracle. A miraculous happening had transformed me from a liability, in a manner of speaking, to an asset by which many of my fellow human beings stood to benefit. Instead of being a slave to alcohol, I had suddenly become a vessel through which countless persons could receive the encouragement and incentive to be freed from the living hell that is the lot of those hopelessly addicted to this socially-accepted drug.

Being in the Program has been a wonderful experience for me. One that is unequaled by any and every aspect of my life prior to my own deliverance. I derive much joy in my endeavors to share with others some of my own ghoulish experiences during those years of my addiction. I have been in the Program about 13 years at the time of this writing and haven't had much, if any, desire to monkey around with booze during that time.

I sometimes catch myself reflecting, inwardly, as to how and why my drinking habit came to be and why I didn't heed the danger signals that were there for my benefit, had I observed them from my childhood.

Admittedly, there were always people around me that drank alcohol to one degree or another. As I think back over the years, there were a few who let drinkin' get the best of them, as it did me, but not many. The big shots, who became a regular aspect of our lives, all drank. So drinking with them seemed the proper thing to do.

Now, drinking with these friends was not entirely to my liking. Most of these guys would put their drink down on the bar, drop in some olives or maraschino cherries and wind up with a regular fruit salad.

That was not my way of drinkin'! I'd put a pint in my pocket when I went to the bar to "have a drink with the boys." I would slip into the back room and take a good swig out of my pint bottle, then go back to the bar for another "sip" with my drinkin' buddies. Pretty soon, I had gotten a full head of steam, and I'd still be drinkin'. That was my way of drinkin' and I asked my sponsor about this one time.

"Gordon," I said, "how come is it that some people can walk into a bar and buy a drink, drink half of it and tell a story or two and walk back out, leavin' half of their drink sittin' there? These people drove me crazy, y'know."

"Well, Edgar," he answered, "these guys are social drinkers."

"Maybe that's what I was, a social drinker," I said. "If you'll have a drink, so shall I...two or three of them."

One incident that occurred in my work with Alcohol Anonymous will always stand out as being one of my most satisfying involvements in helping an addict find his way back to a meaningful life. I had been invited to address a group at a large, well-known clinic in Minnesota. At the end of my speech, which I prefer to refer to as a chat, a gentleman came up to me, obviously with something on his mind.

"Mr. Brooks, I'm Doctor so-and-so," this well-dressed fellow introduced himself as he shook my hand. "I have been highly impressed with your talk this evening. I think, perhaps, the right man has finally come along—someone I can talk to about a problem in my life that has reached the dimension of a crisis."

"I am a surgeon," he continued. "Several years ago, I was called in to perform surgery on a patient who had been brought into the emergency department by ambulance following a bad auto accident. Not anticipating anything like this to occur, I had been imbibing in alcoholic beverage to excess. I have been assured by those who assisted me in the operating room that I performed the surgical procedures O.K. The paradox of all this, Mr. Brooks, is that when I got around to sobering up the next day, I had no recollection, whatsoever, of operating on this critically injured person!"

"Tonight, your sharing some of your own experiences with alcohol has convinced me that it is high time I face up to the fact that I am an alcoholic in need of help. And I feel, somehow, that you are just the man who can provide me that help," he concluded.

I spent time with this surgeon and have every reason to believe that this important mission was successful. There have been numerous cases in which I was able to help bring addicts to alcohol out of their bondage but the one I just mentioned will always stand out as a special case, in a class all by itself.

Someone has said that the rewards of good deeds done are built in. In this, I concur wholeheartedly. The good feeling, deep down inside me as I observe some of these people I have been instrumental in helping with their drinking problem, defies description. The Good Book speaks of "the peace that passes understanding" and this phrase comes about as close to describing my "rewards" as anything I can come up with.

You're coo-coo

As the time for us to seriously consider retirement began to appear on the horizon, I found myself giving thought to finding some worthy pursuit to engage in when that time did finally arrive.

I toyed with a half-dozen ideas, all of which failed to measure up to my objective for one reason or another. I had finally decided that we should get into some project that would add a dimension of meaning and happiness to the lives of senior citizens. I was especially interested in those people residing in nursing homes.

Having established this objective as a top priority, I began to kick around some ideas as to how best to accomplish it. It would have to be something that wasn't unduly expensive to do over for an indefinite period of years and something that wouldn't require us to be dependent on a lot of people.

After giving this much thought, Allie and I decided that maybe music was a practical way to go. I had played the drums up until I was about 10 years old, so I thought maybe I could get back into doing that again after all these years.

I had a younger brother out on the west coast who was a band leader. His wife, June, also had a band of her own, as did their son. No doubt about it, they were pretty big in the musical entertainment business.

I called my brother long distance. "Buddy," I said, "would it be possible for Allie and me to come out there and get you and June to help us make some tapes of various styles of music? We are giving serious thought to starting a little two-person band and we would use these tapes for back-up music. I'll play the drums and Allie will accompany with her tambourine while we sing together.

"We're giving thought to going around to the nursing homes and senior citizen centers around here and entertaining these people. What do you think of that idea? Will it work?"

"What do I think about that?" Buddy thundered. "I think it's crazy!"

"You think it's crazy?"

"Yep, I sure do," Buddy responded emphatically.

"Well then," I said, "why don't I call it the Coo-Coo Band?" And that's how the Coo-Coo Band had its beginnings and that's what it's been ever since.

No excuses

I was smoking quite heavily back in those days and with the time approaching for us to make the trip out to my brother's place, I found myself hoarse in the throat.

"Now, if I'm going to have any kind of a voice to sing with when we get out there, I'm going to have to quit smoking," I reasoned. Buddy was used to operating at a high level of performance, and he wouldn't be too happy having me accompany him on the tapes with a raspy voice, y'know.

That's how I finally got around to getting rid of the smokin' habit I'd had since I was a young boy. I quit smokin' the same way I quit drinkin'—right now, with no ifs or ands about it. It took me about two weeks to get rid of the hoarseness in my throat and then Allie and I left for the west coast. We spent about a month making the tapes and then we returned home.

From time to time, I would find myself wanting to reach for a cigarette, but each time I would think, "What the hell is the use to go back to smokin'? I'm so near being perfect now, it would be a shame to mess it up."

Actually, we made two trips out to the west coast to have my brother help us make the tapes. On the first trip, we taped some of my dad's favorite songs—"Sidewalks of New York" and other songs of that vintage.

After our second trip out west to make tapes for our Coo-Coo Band repertoire, I went to town and bought me a set of drums. There just happened to be a young fellow who had advertised a set of drums over in Hibbing, which turned out to be exactly what I wanted. So, I wound up with a very fine set of drums and a good amplifier at a cost of somewhere around $1,500.

It didn't take Allie and me long to get our act together and we commenced entertaining folks in the nursing homes in our area. We would set up our equipment in the social room of the institution and they would bring as may residents in to hear our program as could be readily moved. Now, if you ever want to experience a feeling of fulfillment, we soon learned that this is one way to accomplish it.

It's difficult to describe how it makes one feel

to see elderly people, sitting in wheelchairs with their heads bent down on their chests, suddenly respond to music they were familiar with in bygone days. Perhaps you might notice an observable tapping of their toes in time with the music or the appearance of a faint smile as they lift up their bowed heads to become a part of the world roundabout them once more. One can only speculate what memories they are recalling—precious memories that have lain dormant for a long, long time.

A THOUSAND KISSES

One story I like to tell as a part of our program always draws a laugh from the folks:

It seems like that wife of mine has a birthday on the fourteenth of March every year and last year I went to buy her a present. I looked all over town and couldn't find anything I could afford, so I thought, "O.K., I'll go home and write her a check for a thousand kisses and stick it under the sugar bowl; she'll find that."

So, that's what I did. Then, I went over to the neighbor's house. When I came back she said, "Edgar, what a beautiful gift that was. How did you think of that?"

"Well," I said, "that was easy. Did you find that already?"

She said, "I sure did."

"What did you do with it?" I asked her.

"That good-looking milkman came along and I had him cash it for me!" she answered.

RAY OF SUNSHINE

At first, we intended to limit our volunteer

musical performances to nursing homes in our immediate area. However, as time went on and word about Edgar and Allie's Coo-Coo Band spread, we began receiving solicitations from care centers, hospitals and organizations promoting senior citizen programs of diverse vintage in an ever-expanding periphery across the Iron Range.

During the eight years or so that the Coo-Coo Band has existed, we have played at all the nursing homes from Grand Rapids to Virginia. We have played for dances at the Moose Club in Bovey, many times at the Memorial Building for the senior citizens in Hibbing, and at Hibbing Bennett Park. We are usually someplace on the programs of annual Fourth of July celebrations at Nashwauk, Keewatin and other towns in this vicinity. The Buck Lake Fortieth Reunion, held August 24, 1989, found Edgar & Allie's Coo-Coo Band on the firing line. Ironworld USA, a museum and convention center close to Chisholm, is by far the largest center of its type to be found on the Iron Range, and we have performed there also.

Our musical act hasn't exactly been a "get-rich-quick" venture, nor was it ever intended to be. Our foremost objective was, and still is, to use this as a way of showing our gratitude for the abundant blessings God has granted Allie and me over the entire span of our lives. What better way is there to do this than to be instrumental in bringing a ray of sunshine into lives that are being lived in a restricted environment by reason of advanced age or ill health?

GOLDEN GIRL

(Author's note: This seems a fitting place to

interject Allie's description of a relatively new dimension in her lifestyle.)

Edgar and I are members of the Buck Lake Improvement Club and have been ever since our return to Buck Lake from Minneapolis in 1973. On Dec. 7, 1988, we invited the Golden Girls Hula Dancers to perform at one of our senior citizen gatherings.

After the performance, I talked to Violet Asuma, the instructor of the group. She asked me if I would like to join the group.

"Yes, it sounds like it would be lots of fun," I replied.

We practiced at the Memorial Building in Hibbing and at Violet's house occasionally.

Violet furnished me with a list of songs and what dance procedures we were to follow during each particular song. She also provided me with a tape so I could practice at home.

Our Golden Girl Hula Dancers have performed at numerous schools, nursing homes and senior citizen centers; also at Larson's Barn Dance in Palisade, Minnesota. One day, we danced at three different locations.

We usually have six dancers but occasionally, someone can't make it and we put on our show with whatever number we happen to wind up with at the time. But no matter how many dancers we have, we always have fun!

One time when we were dancing for the senior citizens at the YMCA in Grand Rapids, Violet's hula skirt fell off, leaving her exposed a bit. Edgar was taking pictures of the show, but didn't get that one. His camera had run out of film just before it happened. Probably just as well that it did!

Violet Asuma is a wonderful person to work with and seems to be able to understand that

we seniors do have problems sometimes, which requires much patience on her part, to be sure.

I had to have a hip replacement on March 23, 1990. Then, on Nov. 21, 1990, I had surgery for a hiatal hernia. On May 6, 1991, I had major surgery for my old back problem that had its beginnings with a roller skating accident not long after Edgar and I were married.

This time, the arthritis spurs and a cyst were removed from my spine. My spine was rebuilt with cross pieces of platinum that looked something like a ladder. Blood and bone were taken from my good hip and placed in the space between the cross pieces of platinum to form new bone growth.

"If your back hurts, it's not going to be from the waist down," my surgeon informed me, and he was right about that.

I do experience a lot of pain in my upper

back much of the time. It sometimes hurts so bad I could cry; but I figure it's going to hurt just as much if I stay home, so I take a couple of pain pills and go about our business with the Coo-Coo Band performances or what have you as best I can.

Since my back surgery in 1991, I haven't danced with the Golden Girls Hula Dancers, but hope to resume doing so sometime in 1993.

REFLECTIONS OF...

(As told by Edgar Brooks)

Y'know, it's funny, when you look back over a half-century or more of time, how some things sort of fall into place like the pieces of a big jig-saw puzzle. You can see things that at the time seemed to represent adversities and times of hard testing but which later proved to be an integral part of a master plan that was being worked out all the while.

For instance, take the matter of Allie's sustaining her back injury while roller skating at Hibbing during the early years of our marriage. This injury has resulted in much suffering and incapacitation on Allie's part over the years, but it was her need for back surgery that brought us to Minneapolis back there in the early Fifties. Had we not found ourselves living in Minneapolis, temporarily at first, I wouldn't have taken employment at Brinkton Corporation and later, at Flower City Ornamental Iron Company. And had it not been for the employee cuts that resulted in my being laid off, I probably wouldn't have experimented with the deer-feet gun rack idea that launched our future destiny onto an entirely unanticipated course.

Had I not gotten into the gun rack venture,

Brooks Taxidermy Service, which eventually became one of the foremost taxidermy businesses in the entire world, would never have come into existence. So, it becomes clearer in my mind as I grow older, that a Power greater than our own is constantly at work in our lives from beginning to end. We're just not always aware of it.

For Allie and me, the jig-saw puzzle of our life probably started to be put together when the Big Depression of the Thirties wiped out my father's financial empire. That event resulted in his decision to move our family to Itasca County more than 60 years ago and the myriad of pieces of this incredible jig-saw puzzle have been falling into place ever since.

With this awareness, comes another awareness: The number of pieces yet to be fit into their respective places are growing less in number with each passing year or conceivably, with each passing day. Let's face it, when we hit or surpass that three-quarter-of-a-century mark, the expiration date on our lease on life becomes progressively more imminent. When I reflect on this reality, a certain quotation takes on special meaning for both Allie and me:

"I expect to pass through this life but once;
Therefore, any good that I can do,
Any kindness that I can show,
Let me do it now;
For I shall not pass this way again."

During the past year or two in particular, both of us have had occasion to face reality that the time has come for us to start cutting back on our busy, sometimes hectic Coo-Coo Band schedule. The same thing is happening in this musical entertainment venture that happened to us in the taxidermy business. It's commencing to burgeon out of proportion.

They've got us playin' all over the country. Two weeks ago, we played five days in a row for senior citizens, nursing homes and dances. This week we have just finished playing five days in a row again. We've played for dances and community celebrations of all kinds, not to mention clubs, organizations and reunions. Seems like everything Allie and I get into eventually gets out of hand.

Now, make no mistake about it, our Coo-Coo Band musical entertainment venture has been, and still is, one of the most satisfying, gratifying things we have ever become involved in during our entire lifetime; but...

The distinct click emanating from my portable tape player served notice that the final cassette I had been transcribing had ended before Edgar could complete the sentence he had been dictating. Yet, it was as though I knew exactly, word for word, what his thoughts consisted of at that moment.

"But...We've got to slow down some. Like everything we've ever done in our lives, it's just become too much."

18

Caring touch

On May 31, 1992, my wife and I left our home in Brownsville, Texas by auto for what would be an extensive itinerary through 14 midwestern states. Aside from pit-stops at the homes of relatives residing in five of these states, the occasion for making the trip consisted of our being present at a reunion celebrating the fifty-fifth anniversary of our high school class graduation in Clarion, Iowa; a month-long stay in the vicinity of our former home in far northeast Iowa; and a visit at the home of Edgar and Allie Brooks at Buck Lake about midway through our three-month trip.

Our little Dodge Caravan, loaded to overflowing with personal items that included my word processor, entered the tree-lined driveway leading to their house around 11 a.m. on July 21, 1992.

Because we had been in frequent contact by

long distance telephone during the past 11
months since seeing them last, no barriers of
inhibition were evident upon our arrival, as had
mildly been the case at the time of our prior pit-
stop at Buck Lake in August of 1991. This time,
our coming together was more like "old home
week." A common interest had long since
removed any reservations that otherwise might
have existed.

By this time, considerable work had been
done on the manuscript, but much in the way
correcting dates, details, names and locations
was needed. Most of this necessitated the presence of Edgar and Allie at my elbow, so to
speak. We spent several days working on the
manuscript together and then, later in the week,
we took time out to do some sightseeing.

One highlight was our tour of National Steel
Pellet Company's taconite plant located in nearby Keewatin. Allie's nephew, Richard Peratalo,
who is an employee at the huge complex, proved
himself to be a knowledgeable tour guide,
explaining the intriguing, complicated sequence
of processes involved in the conversion of unre-
fined, low-grade iron ore into small, marble-
sized taconite pellets. The tour was particularly
fascinating to me, as I had been interested in
the taconite epic since its inception several
decades prior.

Early on Sunday morning, all of us piled into
Edgar's pickup truck and headed for Effie to
attend a rodeo. At my request, a side-trip was
taken to Napoleon Lake to pay a brief visit to the
resort Edgar and Allie had built and operated
back in the late Forties and early Fifties, which I
had never seen.

The narrow, unimproved road, leading from
the highway through densely wooded forest
country to the resort, lay much as it had been at

the time Edgar and Allie arrived at Napoleon Lake some 46 years prior.

I could readily empathize with the inner feelings of our hosts as we traversed the sometimes bumpy 13 miles leading to our destination on the north shore of the secluded lake. Memories, long dormant in their minds, were being vividly recalled as we entered the clearing in which several cabins and what appeared to be a large family-sized dwelling were to be seen.

The foundation of a building was still observable down near the edge of the lake. I surmised it to have been the former location of the little combination grocery store and tavern during Edgar and Allie's time there, which had been destroyed by fire several years ago.

Briefly and without alighting from the truck, we conversed with several children and their mother, who were obviously residing in the larger of the buildings, at least during the summer. Edgar's inquiry as to the quality and quantity of bass being caught in the lake met with an enthusiastic affirmative on the part of the children.

"For as long as I can remember, Napoleon has always been one of the best northern lakes around," Edgar volunteered, as he headed back out in the direction from which we had come.

About midway back to the highway, Edgar brought the truck to a halt atop a small, wood-planked bridge spanning a narrow stream of water that meandered lazily through the dense growth of aspens and pine trees all about us.

Leaning over toward the window on the passenger side of the cab, Edgar pointed to a spot in the creek, immediately beyond the east edge of the makeshift bridge.

"Right there's where Harry took the headlong dive into the drink that time," Edgar recalled. "I'll never forget that day as long as I live! All we could see of Harry was his boots sticking straight up out of the water! I guess he would have drowned, for sure, if we hadn't jumped in and pulled him out!" Edgar's hearty laughter filled the interior of the cab as he relived the incident.

It was approaching dusk when we returned to the Brooks' residence, after our having attended the rodeo and stopped at a nice wayside inn for supper. Some preparation to expedite an early departure for the western part of Minnesota the following morning was undertaken and the balance of the evening was spent watching television.

For some time after the rest of the household had retired for the night, I tarried at the table perusing some areas of the manuscript that I felt stood in need of rephrasing and editing. Some time was spent, too, thumbing through the pages of Edgar and Allie's voluminous scrapbook, which had provided the catalyst that triggered my compulsion to write *Back To Buck Lake* back in August of 1991. This was an unusual correlation of newspaper articles, photographs and other communiques of diverse vintage, all relating to the 30 or so years in the taxidermy business and their more recent years with the Coo-Coo Band involvement.

One letter caught my eye. Edgar had told me that on May 15, 1992, during the Senior Options North Expo held at the Duluth Entertainment and Convention Center, he and Allie were presented an award as winners in the Caring Companions Category of the Success Over Sixty observation.

This event was sponsored by the Aging Trust Fund, which is a program of the Northeastern

EDGAR & ALLIE BROOKS POSE WITH ART LINKLETTER, MAY 15, 1992

Minnesota Initiative (NMI) Fund, whose goal is to promote independence, dignity and self-esteem among older adults. Financial support for the variety of imaginative projects, activities and services is provided by the NMI Fund. Art Linkletter was the keynote speaker at the event.

Edgar and Allie were honored for brightening up senior citizen meetings and care centers and hospitals with their musical entertainment programs throughout the Iron Range.

Another item that caught my eye was a full-page spread, complete with pictures, which appeared in the May 3, 1992 issue of the *Hibbing Daily Tribune*. The extensive article, written by Doreen Lindahl, a member of the staff, included pictures and data covering Edgar and Allie's life history from early on to the present time. It was a bang-up job on the part of this talented journalist.

As I reread the myriad of acknowledgements and expressions of appreciation from numerous hospitals, nursing homes and entertainment centers scattered throughout the Iron Range, I found myself embroiled in some rather in-depth reflections.

"What is the underlying impetus that compels some of us to create and maintain scrapbooks portraying various aspects of our respective lives?" I asked myself.

Is it pride of accomplishment? Or is it a manifestation of our subconscious need to maintain a tangible link between the past, which is gone, and the present, which, in actuality, is our only viable possession?

Or is it an instinctive awareness that someday our memories will be undergoing at least a degree of deterioration and that such a collection of memorabilia will serve to help keep these precious memories of a bygone era in our lives intact?

Or is it simply a means of sustaining our sense of self-esteem and self-worth, to some extent?

Perhaps, for some of us at least, these speculative motivations may hold true in their entirety; for others, only in part. And which, if any, of them applied to Edgar and Allie's feeling the need to compile their scrapbook, which, indubitably is a classic?

For me, the message reverberating from its contents is simply stated, "Hey look! This is who we have been and this is who we are! God has blessed us richly and abundantly. We are humbly grateful for His having had His hand upon us all the way, through thick and thin, sometimes without our having been more than vaguely aware of it."

It was nearing midnight when I finally closed the hardcover scrapbook, returning it to its customary place as the centerpiece of the massive, oak dining table. I was reveling anew in the accomplishments and laudable attitude that the documentary attested to so impressively.

Now, it would be my task to perpetuate the spirit of adventure, achievement and accomplishment that this amazing couple has manifested so laudably over the span of half-a-century. Their example serves as an inspiration to the people they touch. Their strong sense of self-responsibility is a stark contrast to the "let George do it" or "the Government will do it for me" attitude that is so prevalent in today's world.

Nine-thirty the following morning found us packed up and ready to head out for parts westward. Our "goodbyes" were exchanged in a mutual awareness that the past six days had been a meaningful time for all of us.

Glancing into the rear-vision mirror of the mini-van as we headed up the gentle incline leading to the road beyond, I observed a scene that will long remain indelibly etched in my memory.

Waddling up out of the lake and crossing the lawn that stretched from the lakeshore to the rear of the house, a flock of wild ducks was converging where Edgar and Allie were tossing handfuls of shelled corn onto the lawn for them to eat. It was obviously a daily ritual these ducks had come to look forward to with eager anticipation, as the practice had become well-established over an extended period of years.

It seemed a fitting climax to the special, set-aside time we had spent as guests in the home of this friendly couple. The rather remarkable sequence of events that had commenced more than 50 years prior to that time, was evolving

into a dimension of unfolding developments
entirely undreamed of during their inception.

BEYOND BUCK LAKE

In the fall of 1992, Edgar and Allie acted
upon a rather monumental decision that had
been pending for some time. With another winter approaching and wanting to escape the
ongoing task of keeping the snow shoveled off
the driveway and expansive parking area on
their lake property, they accepted the offer of a
prospective buyer and moved to a new residence
in Hibbing.

Sometime in January, 1993, I received a long
distance telephone call from them informing me
that they had recently been nominated by members of the Hibbing Senior Citizen's Center for
the roles of king and queen during the upcoming Hibbing Centennial Celebration.

On Feb. 8, I received another call from
Edgar: "Well, Bob, the Brooks' are at it again!"
Edgar's voice came booming over the line. "Allie
has always wanted to crown me and it looks like
she'll finally get the chance to do it! Allie and I
have been officially elected by the Senior
Citizen's Center in Hibbing to be the king and
queen for the upcoming centennial observation.
I suppose we'll ride in the parades, appear in
the parks and at the schools. We haven't been
informed what other functions, if any, we will be
asked to take part in. In any event, this is quite
an honor for us, to be sure."

Somehow, I knew what was coming before
Edgar broke the news of their having been
selected king and queen for the Hibbing
Centennial Celebration. Something inside had
alerted me as to what he was about to
announce. When he actually conveyed the news,

it only served to confirm what I had already suspected was coming.

It seems inevitable that wherever Edgar and Allie's trek through this life chances to take them, new doors of adventure further enhancing their lives will continue to open for them. Coincidence? Mere happenstance? I think not.

As I pondered Edgar's news, some excerpts from the poem, entitled "IF" came to my mind.

"If you can fill each minute
with sixty seconds full of distance run..."

"If you can keep your head when,
all about you, men are losing theirs..."

"If you can walk with kings,
nor lose the common touch..."

During their years of dealing with the public, Edgar and Allie have related to people whose names are to be found in "Who's Who In America" and possibly in the "Guinness Book of Records." Truly, they have "walked with kings," yet never forfeited the "common touch." Never once.

It is for this quality of charisma, this virtue of not having permitted their achievements to disassociate them from the mainstream of humanity, that they should be remembered, long after the physical presence of these two gallant, worthy people has ceased to exist. Viva la Coo-Coo Band!

—*S. LOWELL ROBERTS*

Scrapbook

A RESPECTABLE COLLECTION OF TROPHIES BY BROOKS TAXIDERMY

DEER FAWN MOUNTED FOR SHAWN MARSH OF BUCK LAKE

ARCTIC GRIZZLY MOUNTED FOR THE HIRT BROTHERS OF GRAND RAPIDS

Turkey mounted for Marshall Field's window in Chicago

Mountain goat mounted for Jeff Perrella of Hibbing

AFRICAN RHINOCEROS

MOUNTAIN LION FROM THE WESTERN UNITED STATES

Bighorn sheep from British Columbia

Canadian Lynx

Northern Minnesota bobcat

African warthog

AFRICAN LEOPARD

AFRICAN SABLE

AN $18,000 ALASKAN POLAR BEAR TROPHY

**BROOKS
Taxidermy**
STAR ROUTE 3, BOX 78B
HIBBING, MINNESOTA
55746
(218) 885-2199

SPECIALIZING IN AFRICAN,
ASIAN AND NORTH AMERICAN
WILD GAME, BIRDS & FISH

Taxidermist

Quality Taxidermy . . .

is like buying oats. If you want nice clean, fresh oats, you must pay a fair price. However, if you can be satisfied with oats that have already been through the horse . . .

THAT COMES A LITTLE CHEAPER!

BROOKS TAXIDERMY BUSINESS CARD

Dear Edgar & Allie,

I enjoyed your music at the Our Senior Citizens Banquet on St Pat Day.

I'm Finnish so enjoyed that music very much. Also I like the & Country Western so the whole program was enjoyable.

Hope to hear you again sometime.

Thank you
Elsie Palmer

Thank you for coming and sharing your talents with us. We appreciate you.

Happy Spring!

Residents of Leisure Hills & Activities

Edgar & Allie, *Valentines.*

May all your dreams come true!

Thanks for coming and in this bad weather to play for us.

Senior Nutrition Bunch
Keewatin, Minn
Feb. 15, 1990

FEBRUARY 1, 1990

EDGAR BROOKS
STAR ROUTE HIBBING
NASHWAUK, MINN. 55769

DEAR EDGAR:

ON BEHALF OF ALL THE RESIDENTS OF ITASCA NURSING HOME, WE WOULD LIKE TO TAKE THIS OPPORTUNITY TO "THANK YOU" FOR ALL YOU DO FOR US. OUR LIVES ARE RICHER, FULLER, AND HAPPIER BECAUSE OF YOU. YOU SHARE A MOST PRECIOUS GIFT WITH US: THE GIFT OF YOURSELF.

THANKS AGAIN!

MARIE CAREY,
PRESIDENT

JOSIE CARLSON,
VICE-PRESIDENT

JUNO HOSS,
SECRETARY

Edgar & Ollie
You guys are special
People. We want to thank you
so very much for coming &
Playing for us. You make us
happy & smile. Thanks again.
Kay Olson ☺
(Act Director)
Manor House)

Hi Folks, 3/19/92
I want to thank
you both for the
wonderful job you
did playing and singing
and especially the good
jobs you tried at our
Sr. Citizen Banquet
the head-aching
but good about your
band and everyone
enjoyed it. Hope we
can get you again
some time. Take Care
Best Wishes, Ruth

Range Mental Health Cente[r]
at MESABI REGIONAL MEDICAL CE[NTER]

750 East 34th Street, Hibbing, Minnesota 55746
MENTAL HEALTH SERVICES   (218) 262-1001 MN Wat[s]
CHEMICAL DEPENDENCY SERVICES   (218) 262-1581 MN Wat[s]

December 19, 1991

Edgar and Ailie Brooks
HC 83 Box 78B
Hibbing, MN 55746

Dear Ailie and Edgar,

The giving of ourself is the most precious gift we can give. Each of us is
unique and contributes as an individual as well as a member of a group.
During the last year you have given that gift. Maybe it was your smile, a
story you told or an understanding nod, but you each in your own unique way,
contributed a special gift of self which helped our Adult Day Program be
successful. We thank you for that giving of your time and talents during
the last year.

The clients, staff, and administration of Range Mental Health\Mesabi, Adult
Day Care wish you a joyful holiday season and a Happy New Year!

Sincerely,

Norma Schleppegrell
Norma Schleppegrell,
Director

NS/b:

Happy Holidays!
Pat Lamppa

Thanks for
everything!
Doug

Merry Christmas!
Carmen

Merry Christmas!
Darlene

Season's Greetings

An Equal Opportunity Employer

Back To Buck Lake

March 24, 1992

Senior Options North

ARROWHEAD CENTER
330 CANAL PARK DRIVE
DULUTH, MINNESOTA 55802

Allie & Edgar Brooks
HC 3 Box 78B
Hibbing, MN 55746

Dear Mr. & Mrs. Brooks:

Congratulations! You have been selected as the winner of the Caring
Companions category of the Success Over Sixty Awards. Sponsored
by the Aging Trust Fund, this award is given in recognition of your
outstanding achievement and accomplishments. The Aging Trust Fund
is a program of the Northeastern Minnesota Initiative Fund, whose goal
is to promote independence, dignity, and self-esteem among older adults
by providing financial support for a variety of imaginative projects,
activities, and services.

In addition to the awards ceremony during Senior Options North '92,
you and the other seven award winners will be honored at the Success
Over Sixty Awards luncheon to be held on **Monday, April 20, 1992.**
When your award is presented, you will be given the opportunity to
acknowledge the award. An invitation to the luncheon will be mailed to
you on April 1 and you are welcome to bring a guest.

The awards ceremony will be held during Senior Options North '92 on
Friday, May 15, 1992 at 1:00 p.m. in the DECC Auditorium.
Following the awards ceremony, you will hear a presentation by our
keynote speaker, Art Linkletter. We are also planning a picture-taking
session prior to the ceremony. You and our other award winners will
have the opportunity to have your picture taken with Mr. Lifnkletter.

Prior to the event, I will send you two complimentary tickets and a
copy of the tabloid that will be published in our local newspapers. The
tabloid will familiarize you with Senior Options North '92 and the
planned events. I will also send you more detailed information
regarding the award ceremony.

218/722-5545 or 800-232-0707 (MN Toll Free)   A PROGRAM OF THE ARROWHEAD REGIONAL DEVELOPMENT COMMISSION

292

March 24, 1992
Page Two

Again, my congratulations on your selection as a "Success Over Sixty" award winner. You can be very proud of your accomplishments. We will be sending out a press release on these awards, so you may be contacted for an interview.

I look forward to meeting you at the luncheon on April 20. In the meantime, please call me if you have any questions at (218) 722-5545 or MN TOLL FREE 1-800-232-0707.

Sincerely,

A. Jane Ankrum
Project Coordinator, Senior Options North
Arrowhead Regional Development Commission

Enclosures

c: Marieta Johnson
    Joyce Ranger
    Delores Nolan

OLD TIME AND COUNTRY WESTERN

Edgar and Allie's
COO-COO
BAND

BOOKING ADDRESS   TELEPHONE
                       ...985-3468

If an old man loves a young lady,
That's his business

If a young lady loves an old man,
That's her business

And if you turn this card over,
That's our business

Coo-Coo Band business card

293

Edgar and Allie come full circle to Buck Lake

By DOREEN LINDAHL

Edgar Brooks and Allie Peratalo met sixty-five years ago when they were fifth graders at the Buck Lake School, and they're still going around together.

For the past eight years, the twosome — as Edgar and Allie's Coo-Coo Band — has brought toe tapping entertainment to people of nursing homes

grew until the last year they made them, they did 40,000. That's a lot of work and a lot of deer feet. He said, "I dreamed deer feet."

His expertise in taxidermy gave him a reputation that had people from all over the world coming to have him do their work. On the fourth day, I went to that farmer and asked for a folding chair. He said, 'What do you want that for?' I said I was going to sit on it out on the dike until I shoot a moose. I'd found a trail where one would be coming

President J F

o'clock, I and asked, elbarrow?'

Coo Coo Band keeps toes tapping

by Barb Hendricks

Does a set of drums, a tambourine and a boom box make a band? It does if you add the voices of Edgar and Allie Brooks, both 72 years young, of Buck Lake.

They formed their Coo Coo band and volunteered to entertain the elderly in area nursing homes who need somebody to sing for them, to make them laugh, to help them remember the old days.

Edgar took me down into the basement and he flicked on the light switch. There sitting in the corner was a silver/black set of drums. Beside them was the amplifier which he said he just had repaired. On the other side of the drum set was a big boom box and a cassette-filled table. He turne ored me with a song and funny joke.

A few years ago, Edgar saw an ad i newspaper selling a set of drums. F not played drums since he was 1 old, about 50 years ago, but he bo

the Coo Coo band progr Allie love hearing the lau smiles, the dancing and Edgar said, "It's all wortt an elderly man who has chair with his head hangi lift his head and there o smile, all because he ha favorite songs being pla feel good inside."

"Some dance, other "hairs move to d Allie.

Edgar and and Allie are 'cuckoo' for life

NASHWAUK May 12 1988

Edgar Brooks' life has always been full. Through the years he has traveled, worked hard and rubbed elbows with the great and near-great. Through his taxidermy business in Minneapolis, he worked for famous people like nt Nixon (pheasants), President Lyndon Johnson (a entertainers like Bing Crosby, Vern le (of the Lawrence Welk Show) nt who brought him

about 23 ers and nd the prize catch, He n from the tagged and

A former Buck Lake couple receive achievement award

Allie and Edgar Brooks of Hibbing and former Buck Lake residents were selected th winner of the Caring Co ions category of Over Sixty Spons

Hibbing and former Buck Lake contrib or

a program or

Seniors: They're still successful

Caring companions:
Edgar & Allie Brooks, Hibbing They've brightened up seniors meetings and hospitals with musi and dancing.

He's a partner in the "Coo-C band, playing drums and te' jokes. She's a member of Hula Girls," dancing in Ha' costumes.

Allie Brooks, 76, and band, Edgar, 76, met in fl at an old country schoc Lake, and they've beer and helping friends an fact, a f

ven in outstanding ent and
The Aging Trust Fund is a program of the Northeastern Minnesota Initiative Fund whose goal is to promote independence, dignity and self-esteem among older adults h providing financial support i a variety of imaginativ projects, activities and services

The Brooks' were among nine senior citizens honored at a luncheon recently by Senior Options North and the Aging Trust Fund for their achi ments after passin birthday

booth 76, were the Caring Compan
up senior meetings and hospi tals with dancing and music. Together they form Edgar and Allie's Coo-Coo Band, which provides old time country west em music. Edgar plays drums and tells jokes, and Allie is also member of the Hula Girls.

The couple fifth

tle time for piled up and was people working ould do the

y to the lips of f the excitement est friends are his largie. ng with the shop from until she married and he kept the books and om my other

Local couple wins

Allie and Edgar Brooks of Hibbing and former Buck Lake residents were selected winners of the Caring Companions category the Success Over Sixty A cently sponsored h Trust Fund Th recogniti em

North and their

Edgar and Allie take Hibbing

Edgar and Allie Brooks of Buck Lake moved to Hibbing from Buck Lake five months ago. Today, they are the king and queen of the Hibbing Sr. Citizens.

"Allie always wanted to crown me and now she finally can," Edgar said of the honor.

The coronation ceremony took place Wednesday, Feb. 17 at the Hibbing Sr. Citizen's Clubroom in the Hibbing Memorial Building.

The event is part of the choosing of a Frolic, which

Winter Frolic Queen from a group of young women vying for the title, and a Titan of Taconite from among a list of Hibbing dignitaries. The event also includes a treasure hunt. Winter Frolic royalty will ride in parades and represent Hibbing on special occasions. This is a big year for Hibbing as the city celebrates it's centennial year. Edgar and Allie Brooks are well-known throughout the area for their entertaining "Edgar and Allie's Coo-Coo Band," featur-

BROOKS/To back page
ie's Coo-Co provides old time stern music.

294